Restaurateurs and Innkeepers

by
Irene M. Franck
and
David M. Brownstone

A Volume in the
Work Throughout History Series

Facts On File
New York • Oxford

RESTAURATEURS AND INNKEEPERS

Copyright © 1989 by Irene M. Franck and David M. Brownstone

Library of Congress Cataloging-in-Publication Data

Franck, Irene M.
    Restaurateurs and innkeepers / by Irene M. Franck and David M.
Brownstone.
        p.   cm. — (Work throughout history)
    Bibliography: p.
    Includes index.
    Summary: Explores the role throughout history of occupations
related to food, including bakers and millers, brewers, grocers,
dairy operators, waiters, winemakers, and others.
    ISBN 0-8160-1451-5
    1. Restaurateurs—Juvenile literature. 2. Hotelkeepers—Juvenile
literature. 3. Food industry and trade—Employees—Juvenile
literature. 4. Food industry and trade—History—Juvenile
literature. 5. Hotels, taverns, etc.—History—Juvenile literature.
[1. Food industry and trade—History. 2. Occupations—History.]
I. Brownstone, David M. II. Title. III. Series.
TX910.3.F73 1988
641'.023—dc19   88-11127

British CIP data available on request

Printed in the United States of America

10 9 8 7 6 5 4 3 2 1

Contents

Preface v

Introduction vii

Bakers and Millers 1
Brewers 19
Butchers 23
Confectioners 39
Cooks 45
Costermongers and Grocers 59
Dairy Operators 67
Distillers 77
Fishmongers 83
Innkeepers 87
Poulterers 99
Prostitutes 103
Restaurateurs 131
Waiters 147
Winemakers 151

Suggestions for Further Reading 159

Index 163

Titles in the *Work Throughout History* series

Artists and Artisans
Builders
Clothiers
Communicators
Financiers and Traders
Harvesters
Healers
Helpers and Aides
Leaders and Lawyers
Manufacturers and Miners
Performers and Players
Restaurateurs and Innkeepers
Scholars and Priests
Scientists and Technologists
Warriors and Adventurers

Preface

Restaurateurs and Innkeepers is a book in the multi-volume series, *Work Throughout History*. Work shapes the lives of all human beings; yet surprisingly little has been written about the history of the many fascinating and diverse types of occupations men and women pursue. The books in the *Work Throughout History* series explore humanity's most interesting, important, and influential occupations. They explain how and why these occupations came into being in the major cultures of the world, how they evolved over the centuries, especially with changing technology, and how society's view of each occupation has changed. Throughout we focus on what it was like to do a particular kind of work—for example, to be a farmer, glassblower, midwife, banker, building contractor, actor, astrologer, or weaver—in centuries past and right up to today.

Because many occupations have been closely related to one another, we have included at the end of each article references to other overlapping occupations. In preparing this series, we have drawn on a wide range of general works on social, economic, and occupational history, including many on everyday life throughout history. We consulted far too many wide-ranging works to list them all here; but at the end of each volume is a list of suggestions for further reading, should readers want to learn more about any of the occupations included in the volume.

Many researchers and writers worked on the preparation of this series. For *Restaurateurs and Innkeepers*, the primary researcher-writer was David G. Merrill; Douglass L. Brownstone and Hayden Carruth also wrote parts of this volume. Our thanks go to them for their fine work; to our expert typists, Shirley Fenn, Nancy Fishelberg, and Mary Racette; to our most helpful editors at Facts On File, first Kate Kelly and then James Warren, and their assistants Claire Johnston and later Barbara Levine; to our excellent developmental editor, Vicki Tyler; and to our publisher, Edward Knappman, who first suggested the *Work Throughout History* series and has given us gracious support during the long years of its preparation.

We also express our special appreciation to the many librarians whose help has been indispensable in completing this work, especially to the incomparable staff of the Chappaqua Library—director Mark Hasskarl and former director Doris Lowenfels; the reference staff, including Mary Platt, Paula Peyraud, Terry Cullen, Martha Alcott, Carolyn Jones, and formerly Helen Barolini, Karen Baker, and Linda Goldstein; Jane McKean, Caroline Chojnowski, and formerly Marcia Van Fleet, and the whole circulation staff—and the many other librarians who, through the Interlibrary Loan Network, have provided us with the research tools so vital to our work.

Irene M. Franck
David M. Brownstone

Introduction

Restaurateurs and Innkeepers is a book about the people who meet the public's needs and desires for food, drink, shelter, and personal comfort. For many people throughout history, such needs have often been met in the home. But, especially in places with large populations and frequent travelers, professionals gradually emerged to respond to some of people's needs and desires.

Bread has been the mainstay of humans for thousands of years. So it is not surprising that *bakers* and *millers* were found in very early populations, and continue to be important today. Grain was brought to the miller, who ground it into a more usable form, as flour or meal. Throughout much of history, many people made their own bread. But even so, people too poor to have ovens often brought their prepared dough to shops to be baked.

But bakers began more and more to make bread, cakes, and similar products from scratch, directly for sale to the public. Other specialists called *confectioners* focused on making candies and other fancy sweet goods for the public. While breads, cakes, and candies are often made in huge factories today, cities and even many small towns still have at least one baker and sometimes a candy-maker.

Milk, cheese, and other dairy products have also formed an important part of the human diet for thousands of years. Many people kept family cows—even in cities—and made their own dairy products. But *dairy operators* came to specialize in providing such products to the public. Many kept a stable of milk-producing animals and sold milk to customers fresh from the cow or prepared the dairy products nearby. In modern times, dairies have become large-scale affairs, gathering milk from farmers for hundreds of miles around.

Vegetables and fruits, too, were often grown by individuals in their private "kitchen gardens." But many farmers grew fruits and vegetables in large amounts for sale to the public. Some brought their produce directly to market themselves. But, especially as cities expanded, other people took over the job of bringing the produce to the public. *Costermongers* brought vegetables and fruits to the cities on carts, often driving through the streets to sell their goods. *Grocers*, on the other hand, set up small and later larger shops to sell this produce—and gradually many other foods and products as well.

Meat, poultry, and fish were also important foods, and called for their own specialists. In the days when country people raised their own animals for food, *butchers* often traveled the countryside. If a farmer wanted a cow, pig, or other animal killed and cut up for food, the butcher was often the expert employed to do the job. Increasingly, butchers bought live animals, took them to their shops for slaughter, and cut them up for sale to their customers. *Poulterers* did much the same for various kinds of fowl, including chickens, ducks, and turkeys. Similarly, *fishmongers* have long bought fish of all sorts from fishers, then sold them either directly to the public or to restaurants. Specialists like these still operate, but far fewer than before. Today much of the butcher's, poulterer's, and fishmonger's work takes place in a factory setting.

Alcoholic beverages also were often made at home, but increasingly became the province of specialists. The oldest of these were the *brewers* who have been making beer for thousands of years—as some small pub owners still do today, when most brewing is done in massive factories. *Winemakers* have not quite so long a history, but winemaking became a major industry. By a few centuries before Christ, the early Greeks were exporting wine in large quantities around the Mediterranean, and it was they who introduced winemaking to France and Spain. *Distillers* came a little later, since distilling techniques were not developed in the Mediterranean world until two to three centuries before Christ. Since then distillers have been making brandies, whiskies, and other such alcoholic beverages for public sale.

Other professionals—*cooks*—prepared food for others to eat. In the homes of the rich and the royal, cooks specialized in making fine food, especially for banquets and feasts. For centuries, most cooks were employed by others, but some opened their own restaurants, becoming *restaurateurs*. The most notable of these were French cooks who, after the French Revolution of 1789, found themselves out of work, and went into business on their own. Serving the food in these restaurants were a new set of specialists: *waiters*. As restaurants came to serve a better class of customers, waiters came into the public eye and had to learn a complex set of skills. Other, far less respected cooks provided simpler fare to the public from small cookshops, stands, or carts—as food vendors still do today—in cities and along roadsides. Waiters in such places sometimes double as part-time rough cooks.

Closely related to restaurateurs are *innkeepers*. For centuries, innkeepers provided shelter for travelers on the road, and tavernkeepers sold alcoholic drinks the public. In some periods taverns and inns offered little or no food—though a guest might request that the innkeeper cook a piece of meat bought specially from a butcher. Only in modern times have innkeepers and tavernkeepers often come to be restaurateurs as well.

For many centuries, inns and taverns generally had bad reputations—and for good reason. Guests were often thrown together into a common room, to sleep on hard, flea-filled beds of straw. Among their fellow guests were often robbers and thieves, out to strip travelers of their possessions. *Gamblers* were often found there, and so were *prostitutes*. In fact, many restaurateurs, tavernkeepers, and innkeepers routinely employed prostitutes to serve their guests. The work of prostitutes has been legalized and controlled by governments in some parts of the world throughout history. But most prostitutes have traditionally operated illegally and with little or no respect or status. Many continue to work, as of old, on their own or in small groups, often in bars or hotels.

Restaurants and inns have improved their reputations considerably in the last century or two. Though travelers are still wise to be wary when eating, drinking, or sleeping away from home, many modern hotels and motels provide rather safe, clean, and sometimes even luxurious accommodations. And many modern restaurants serve a large and demanding group of customers, interested in fine food.

Change has come to other food providers, too. As food more often has been prepared in massive factories, customers have begun to long for fresher, better, less "mass-produced" food. The result has been a revival in specialty food shops, sometimes independently owned, sometimes as part of a large supermarket.

Bakers and Millers

Since the earliest times, people have baked breads and biscuits to sustain themselves and their families. For centuries, bread has been considered the "staff of life" because it is—in its natural, whole, and unprocessed form—an extremely nutritious food containing vitamins, minerals, and roughage necessary for good health. Indeed, for many groups of people throughout history, bread and cereal have been the main part of their diet, the foods they depended on to stay alive.

Baking itself is an ancient form of food preparation that was carried on primarily in the home until the modern era. Nonetheless, there have long been professional *bakers* who have sold their breads and related goods to governments, travelers, private households, and commercial dining houses. Milling—the processing and grinding of raw grain into a workable flour—and baking have often been done by the same person. Only in modern times have baker and *miller* become separate professions.

Most Egyptian farms produced barely enough food for the people who farmed them, but small granaries were maintained for the production of bread and beer, the mainstays of the Egyptian diet. Barley and wheat particularly were cultivated toward these ends, and some *farmers* ground their own flour and baked bread commercially. Most of the professional baking was done by government employees who worked the private bakeries of kings and nobles. Public ovens were often made available for use by urban dwellers and were usually supervised by attending officials. In some cases people could bring their own flour to these ovens, where government bakers would make it into bread for a fee. The baker and the *brewer* were frequently the same person, and bakery-breweries are known to have existed as early as 2000 B.C.

Bakers were important in the Egyptian concept of life since they worked with the grain that had been nourished by the revered Nile River, the grain that was considered a sure sign of the gods' mercy on the people. Fertility and religious rites were serious business, for they were believed to have some influence on whether the divine powers granted a bountiful grain harvest. Once granted, the grain then had to be transformed into a more edible form for human consumption. This was the job of the baker. The first professionals in their trade, as far as we know, these bakers also played an essential role in the Egyptian view of death. They were kept busy baking loaves for tombs, so that the dead might be well supplied for their journey into the life beyond. Tomb breads could also be used as offerings to the gods and as prayerful symbols of life in the world of the dead. Since their work was so important, Egyptian bakers developed a rather elevated view of their profession.

When the Egyptian empire declined, the Assyrian armies who conquered portions of it were delighted to count Egyptian bakers and brewers as valuable conquests. These were quickly put to work teaching their craft to Assyrian apprentices as well as producing loaves for the Assyrian armies and for the Assyrian gods. Bakers were soon common throughout the ancient world. In Babylonia, where they first became *shopkeepers*, their profession was highly ranked, on the same level as *diviners* and *physicians*. Indeed, they played analmost sacred role in the daily "feeding of the gods," a ritual practiced throughout Mesopotamia.

In earlier times, grain was ground into flour using a laborious mortar-and-pestle technique, in which a small rounded tool called a pestle was rolled inside a cupped bowl called a mortar in order to crush and pulverize small amounts of grain. Small farms would continue to use this technique for a long time to come. During the Golden Age of Athens, large farms were using millstones—huge stones shaped like cylinders—which were rolled against each other to grind grain into flour.

Millstones were a great improvement over the time-consuming mortar-and-pestle technique, but grinding grain was still a rough job. Many of the bakers and millers of ancient Greece were *slaves*. The miller employed only the worst slave boys—or those being punished for one reason or another—in this thankless task. Slave girls were responsible for gathering the milled grain as it rolled out from the huge stones, which were pushed back and forth by the boys. The work was monotonous as well as backbreaking, and laborers would frequently try to keep from thinking of their misery by chanting encouraging mill songs, such as this popular one:

Grind, mill, grind
For Pittacus did grind—
Who was king over great Mytilene

Millers ground flour fresh for daily use, and they often baked their own breads, using closely supervised slave labor. Bread was essential to the Greek diet, and starvation a constant threat. Since Greece was able to supply only a small proportion of the grain necessary for this critical industry, exports from Greek ports on the Black Sea were heavily relied upon. So desperate was the situation that the Athenian statesman Demosthenes once had to declare the following order:

> It shall not be lawful for any Athenian or any *metic* [a foreigner with no Greek citizenship] in Attica, or any person under their control (neither slave nor freedman) to lend out money on a ship which is not commissioned to bring grain to Athens.

Millers and bakers obviously held a key position in the Athenian economy.

Breads were sold daily in Greek marketplaces, like the famous Agora in Athens. People shopped there every day, since food could not be preserved for long. Only men did the shopping; gentlemen usually sent a trusted slave or servant to do the job for them. *Vendors* were almost always men, except in the case of the bakery goods stalls. Here were to be found old women shrewdly bargaining for every last penny that might be gained from the sale of one of the loaves that they had helped produce the day before. They baked and sold all kinds of loaves. Slender and convenient shapes were common, but the large cylindrical ones were the most popular.

In an age free from advertising and other subtler sales techniques, the women yelled at the crowds of shoppers to buy their loaves at bargain prices. No prices were ever set in the Agora, and quibbling and bartering were routine. The women tried especially hard to attract servants as customers. Servants often bought many large loaves for their masters, who might be entertaining dinner guests that evening at a symposium—a very common sort of dinner party, usually accompanied by stimulating intellectual discussion. By noon, shopping at the Agora was over and the bakery, along with all the other makeshift stalls, was closed up until the next day. The women who ran the stalls returned to help at the mill or in the kitchen, where new loaves were being prepared for the following day.

In ancient Rome, bakeries were found in all the marketplaces. Many of these were established shops, where bakers lived and sold their goods directly from their homes. Nobles and wealthy businessmen had private bakehouses at their residential quarters; they frequently hired head bakers to supervise staffs of slaves. There were also a great many public bakeries and government bakeshops, where people could either buy bread or bring their raw grain for processing. They could then return home with flour or breads at a reduced price. The government bakeshops, like many large commercial bakeries, were situated next to grist mills so that millers and bakers could work side by side.

In the days of the Roman Republic, millers were responsible for pounding, cleansing, and processing raw grain into flour. The miller was crucial to the public welfare even during the Imperial period, since Rome had to import large portions of its wheat. By the second century B.C., most millers had also become bakers, be-

Bakers and millers often occupied the same quarters, as here at Pompeii. (From Museum of Antiquity, *by L.W. Yaggy and T.L. Haines, 1882)*

coming the first of the professions involved in the mass production of food. Large kitchens at the bakeries were staffed with scores of slaves to work the ovens and knead the dough, and with *foremen* or *supervisors* to oversee their progress and efficiency. The millstones were increasingly worked by donkeys or mules, blindfolded so that they would not feast on the grains as they ground them. This practice increased production, as the Roman Empire grew larger and the mouths to feed multiplied. Sometimes a man was strictly a professional miller, sometimes strictly a baker, but very often he was both.

By 100 B.C. there were 258 bakeshops in Rome alone. So important was the profession to the expanding empire that the emperor Trajan undertook the establishment of the world's first baking school and granted full citizenship rights to people who set up bakeries. During the first century A.D. the profession was temporarily thrown into chaos when the cruel and irrational emperor Caligula seized control of all the beasts of burden, which had by then become essential to power the heavy millstones. In succeeding years, bakers and millers developed methods for harnessing waterpower to turn the mill wheels. This proved to be a problem, however, when rivers ran too low to reach the waterwheels. Systems were then devised whereby mills were mounted on floating rafts or boats, so that business could go on undisturbed even during severe droughts. Realizing the importance of the millers and bakers to the welfare of Rome, the Goths temporarily paralyzed the Empire in the sixth century A.D. by cutting off water supplies that powered the mills.

Roman bakers sold a wide variety of breads, but the most common was the two-inch-thick flat loaf. A cheap bread of coarse grain (*panis sordis*) was sold to the peasants, while a finer type (*panis secandus*) was typically sold to upper-class customers. The finest and sweetest of all was the *siligineous*, which was sold usually to gentlemen who were entertaining dinner guests for the evening—as was common in a time when restaurants and taverns were generally reserved for the dregs of society. Even pastries and cakes were made at the Roman bakeshops, as bakers began to apply their skills to make more than simply breads.

In the later days of the Roman Empire, a great many millers and bakers were employed by the emperor to prepare flour and later breads for public handouts (*annona*). At first these were given only to the poor, but as time went on the *Frumetary Lists* of those eligible for public doles of bread and grain increased astronomically. Even gentlemen went to the government bakeshops for their regular handouts. Teams of bakers were kept busy day and night supplying this bread. Not all bakers pursued their trade full time, however. Throughout the pages of Roman history we read about those who were "school masters in the morning; corn grinders at night; and braziers' hammers day and night."

The Middle Ages was a time of great famine in the Western world. There were no fewer than twenty serious famines in Europe between 857 and 957 A.D. Diseases caused by improperly handled or contaminated food made this sad situation even worse. In 857 A.D., for example, there was a widespread and disastrous outbreak of ergotism in the Rhine River Valley. Ergotism is a terrible disease that results from the eating of grains contaminated with a deadly virus known as ergot, which contains twenty poisons including the hallucinogen lysergic acid diethylamide (LSD). Rye is particularly susceptible to this type of contamination, and poisoned rye flour in baked breads killed thousands of people during this epidemic. In the 10th century A.D. Spanish wheat fields were virtually laid bare by a violent outbreak of wheat rust. The rust parasites that infested and diseased years of wheat harvests had been carried into Spain by the Arabs on the harmless-looking barberry bush. Massive starvation resulted as bread shortages were felt even by the great landed nobility.

Because of widespread famine and food poisoning of various sorts, medieval bakers came under more government scrutiny and quality control than had their ancient counterparts. Besides government inspections, bakers had to worry about guild regulations concerning both price-fixing and the internal affairs of the industry. Bakers had organized themselves into guilds to protect themselves from foreign and uncontrolled competition, but many a bread maker later complained that his greatest competition had become the guild itself. Among the guild rules that bakers resented was one that declared a maximum amount of yeast that could be added to a single loaf of bread. The practice of "raising" the breads beyond reasonable limits brought in greater profits for bakers, of course, since a cake of yeast was much cheaper than precious grain flours. But the practice had gotten so out of hand that bakers had earned a rather scandalous reputation and the industry as a whole was suffering as a result. The yeast rule was aimed at restoring the public's faith in bakers, but the purpose of some other guild regulations is less clear. For instance, if a loaf was deemed to be less than perfectly round, it had to be removed from the shop.

Although the long handle allows this baker to keep some distance from the fire, he still wears minimal clothing. (By Jost Amman, from The Book of Trades, *late 16th century)*

Bakers' prices—based on the weight of the loaf—were legally fixed by the government in an attempt to prevent starvation and the black marketing of loaves. Bakers were also obliged to affix their seals to each loaf they produced for sale. This was to prevent one from cheating his customers on the weight of the bread sold. These rules did not stamp out cheating in the bakeries, but they had considerable effect. An offender caught cheating on weight was generally locked in a pillory—a wooden framework, generally set in a public place, into which the head and hands were locked for a specified time—with his underweight loaf tied around his neck; frequently he was carted in a wagon through the poorest sections of town. This was certainly poor publicity for his establishment, and the baker could consider himself lucky if he sustained only slight bodily harm from the objects thrown at him during the procession through an unfriendly neighborhood.

Of course some daring souls always refused to be intimidated by rules and laws. They were careful to be kind to their hired laborers, lest their illegal activities be reported to the local authorities by a disgruntled *doughboy*. Few had more to fear than the London baker named John Brid, who made a regular practice of cheating his customers. In 1327 he had a small trapdoor cut into the countertop where customers placed the home-prepared dough that they wanted baked in Brid's oven. Brid occupied his client in conversation while one of his workers sitting under the trapdoor "piecemeal and bit by bit craftily withdrew some of the dough aforesaid" from the bottom of the loaf. Brid was finally caught, however; his accuser claimed that through this ploy he had stored up considerable amounts of good dough, "falsely, wickedly and maliciously; to the great loss of all his neighbors and persons living near!"

The medieval baker did a hearty business, all told. Among the most popular items for sale were bread trenchers, which were used as dinner plates for many years before they were finally replaced by depressed wooden slabs. The trenchers were thick squares of hard bread with an indented surface into which food could be placed. After the meal, the trencher itself was eaten; frequently the diner would use more than one trencher per meal, if the original one became too soggy to continue with. At wealthy tables, used trenchers were sometimes passed on to the servants.

Probably the happiest bakers of the time were those fortunate enough to be privately employed by a king or noble. In times of famine—which was virtually a way of life—these bakers did not have to concern themselves with trying to sell loaves to a hungry but impoverished public. Moreover, they did not need to worry about whether or not they could obtain grain and flour to carry on their trade, since the nobles and kings were the first to be provided for, while many a public baker went without and starved along with the rest of the good citizens.

Millers at this time were rather free and independent spirits, not tied to guild rules as most other artisans were. They had a reputation for boldness and vulgar earthiness, like the miller in *The Canterbury Tales*, whom

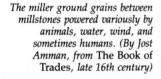

The miller ground grains between millstones powered variously by animals, water, wind, and sometimes humans. (By Jost Amman, from The Book of Trades, *late 16th century)*

Chaucer labeled a gossip and a buffoon, and whose tale was openly bawdy.

Mills gradually became urbanized during the later Middle Ages, with the great growth of towns throughout Europe, though most villages also had their mills. *Burghers, bishops*, and other highly esteemed gentlemen took to the business of milling again. They usually owned the mills, which were located on their estates and riverfront properties, and hired professional millers to supervise the chore of grinding and packaging the grain. Many mills were floated on the hulls of boats to adapt to changing water levels. Although waterpower was the primary source of energy used in rotating or sliding the millstones, animals were usually used for this purpose when the river or canal waters froze. Many a miller was assigned to fishing—a profitable enterprise in itself—during off-hours, when there was no grain to grind, therefore adding even more to the wealth of the landed mill owner.

Although baking remained a solid profession into modern times, most people right up to the 20th century baked their own bread at home. In most cases the woman of the household did the family's baking, but the kitchens of the wealthy employed bakers who lived in and complemented the staffs of *cooks* and *pantry maids*. Baking for rich households remained, as in the Middle Ages, more profitable and secure than owning a public shop; and the surroundings were certainly more pleasant than hot oven shops in busy merchant squares. Gentlewomen of 17th-century European country estates supervised nearly self-sufficient homesteads. They had millers who churned and ground their meal at the mills of the estate, and bakers who made it into bread loaves and cakes for the household of masters, slaves, and employed freemen servants. (Sometimes they would make the bread at home but bake it at a baker's oven or in a shared village oven.) Slaves were used extensively in the American South to provide the labor at plantation bakehouses. At the great English estates of the landed lords, there were different ranks to which bakers could be promoted. In 1662 Patrick Lambe was appointed the "youngest child of pastry" in the royal kitchen. After 23 years of faithful service at that post, he was promoted to "Second Master Cook and Yeoman of the Pastry"—a post that earned him a hefty annual salary of £130, as well as free room and board in one of the greatest courts in the world.

Commercial bakers continued to serve the general population, although people of social standing would not lower themselves to eat the products of such an establishment. The first commercially baked bread in America appeared in 1640. On the European Continent, the sale of wheat and the commercial baking of bread continued to be limited and placed under strict price controls because of persistent recurrences of starvation. The hoarding of grain or baked loaves by bakers, who would sometimes wait for prices to increase in times of food shortage, was illegal and sometimes punishable by death.

During the 18th century bakers found new places of employment in the increasingly popular inns and large taverns. The best bakers could hope for assignments at a royal court or at the estate of a gentleman. The next best could hope to work at an inn. Public bakers were finding better markets, too, as society slowly became more urban and fewer people had their own ovens for baking at home. The space next to a bakery was prime for renting, because

These workers carry out the various steps in the baking process, from kneading to removing from the oven. (From Diderot's Encyclopedia, *late 18th century)*

tenants could take advantage of the heat from the back of the baker's oven; bath operators, for example, vied for this free source of heat for their water—while bakers complained in vain.

American millers were in constant demand and were well paid by landowners, who owned grist mills but needed someone to supervise their operation. Many a mill owner used his grist mill as a lumber mill as well. Millers, then, often doubled as *sawyers*—people who saw wood. Mill owners in America usually were men of at least modest wealth, since a certain capital investment was required to "open shop." Robert Carter of Virginia had to pay a whopping £1,450 for his Revolutionary era mill, but it paid him back quickly by grinding 25,000 bushels of wheat per year. Mill owners then could well afford to pay millers well, and the miller's economic and social standing was relatively high. In 1783, in Connecticut, the average amount on which workers in general had to pay taxes was £33. In contrast, millers—being more prosperous—had to pay taxes on amounts ranging from £50 to £146.

During the Industrial Revolution, as people increasingly moved away from relatively self-sufficient country living to urban areas, grain merchants, millers, and bakers all stood to profit. Even the middle-class gentry began to buy from commercial bakers. In the 1830's newspaper advertisements began to appear for such things as "Biscuits and Cakes For Funerals, offered by Robert Gilpin, Sankey Street, Warrington (England). Considering the nature of the commodity, it is not surprising that Gilpin chose to include in his notice that such biscuits could be "Made on the Shortest Notice."

More commoners and gentlemen began to purchase flour rather than grinding their own, and even royal households followed suit. A Victorian packaging label on corn-flour sacks devised by William Polson and Company bore a picture of Queen Victoria herself; underneath it was claimed that Polson's Company enjoyed the distinction of being "Manufacturers to the Queen." American grain merchants used a more earthy appeal. One retail-sack label of the 1850's pictured a family seated at breakfast. The father asks the oldest son: "Where did you get this nice buckwheat?" The answer: "I got it at Sperling's, of course." The youngest son chimes in, "It's tip top," to which the gleeful maid adds, "Isn't it nice [pan] cakes?"

Bakers worked much as they had for centuries, although a few mechanical devices had been added to their trade. An early 16th-century *Book of Trades* pictures a commercial bakery in action. All the laborers wear kitchen caps, and no fewer than thirteen steps—apparently carried out by thirteen separate

In larger mills, work proceeded on several levels. (From Diderot's Encyclopedia, *late 18th century)*

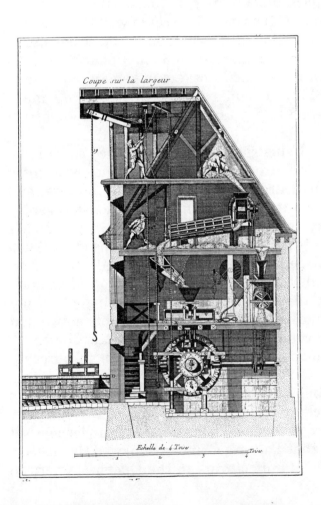

Coupe sur la largeur

Echelle de 4 Tour

laborers—are followed. The following passage gives further details on the picture:

The Mysterie and Trade of Baking

All services that to the Baker's Trade
Or mysterie belong, be here displaid,
Which my rude Arts in order shall recount,
And those in number to thirteen amount,
Being (how ere such Tradesmen used to coozen
In their scale measure) just a Baker's dozen.
First Boulting, Seasoning, Casting up, and Braking,
Breaking out dowe, next Weighing, or weight making
(Which last is rarely seene), then some doe Mould;
This Cuts, that Seales and Sets up, yet behold
The seasoner Heating, or with Barin fires
Preparing the oven as the case requires;
One carrying up, the Heeter peeleth on
And playes the Setter, who's no sooner gone
But the hot mouth is Stopt, so to remaine
Untill the setter drawes all forth againe.
Thus bakers make and to perfection bring,
No less to serve the Beggar than the King,
All sorts of Bread, which being handled well,
All other food and Cakes doth farre excell.
Let Butchers, Poultrers, Fishmongers contend
Each in his own trade, in what he can Defend,
Though Flesh, Fish, Whitemeat, all in fitting season,
Nourish the body, being used with reason,
Yet no man can deny (to end the strife)
Bread is worth all, being the staff of life.

Bakers of the 19th century were popular primarily in the large cities. They played an important role in feeding the new class of factory workers. During the American Civil War, a group of bakers were employed to set up ovens under the Senate chambers in the Capitol building in Washington, D.C., to produce life-sustaining loaves for the Union troops.

Commercial baking was a mixed blessing, however, as became clear with recognition of the widespread adulteration of bread. A major controversy was touched off when investigative reports noted that commercial bread doughs were freely flavored by the steady flow of perspiration streaming down the unwashed arms of overworked, underpaid, half-naked doughboys, who labored in intensely hot kitchens. Most commercial bread, it was reported in 1820, was mixed with alum, a metallic substance used in medicines and dyes. In 1845 it was discovered that most London bread contained large quantities of plaster of Paris. Both alum and plaster were used to make dark bread look whiter, therefore increasing its popularity.

The irony of this new popularity of "white" bread was that its whiteness resulted from the stripping of the bran and wheat germ (endosperm) that had made the bread so nutritious. Without those parts of the grain intact, the bread was "finer and more delectable"—but also less nutritious. The practice of processing the nutrients out of grain—using a milling process developed in Hungary in the 1840's—was attacked eloquently as early as 1857 by Eliza Acton. In her *English Bread-Book* she urged women to bake at home and avoid dealings with commercial bakers at all costs, or else risk their families' physical well-being and health. Her pleas went largely unheeded. In 1910 only 10 percent of the loaves consumed in the United States were bought from commercial bakeries; today that figure has risen to a startling 95 percent.

Most modern bakers and millers work in large factory-like, mass-production operations. Much of the drudgery work that once was done by hand is now done by large machines. Large conveyor racks with rollers move bread rolls along at a rapid clip, until they are dropped into bags or other packages; mechanical pickers wrap or package breads; and even the kneading of dough is usually done by machine. Some bakers, however, still make their products by hand in the back of their shops, retail them at front counters, and wholesale them to restaurants and hotels. In addition to bread, modern bakers also make cakes, muffins, cookies, pies, and many other sweets that once were made mostly by *confectioners*. Doughnuts have been a popular baked item since World War I, when the American Salvation Army handed them out freely to the poor. Some bakery shops now bake only doughnuts.

Bakers and millers are both closely controlled by governments today, regarding weights, prices, fair practices, and flagrant adulteration.

For related occupations in this volume, *Restaurateurs and Innkeepers*, see the following:
Brewers
Confectioners
Cooks
Costermongers and Grocers
Innkeepers
Restaurateurs

For related occupations in other volumes of the series, see the following:
in *Builders*:
Carpenters
in *Financiers and Traders*:
Merchants and Traders
in *Harvesters*:
Farmers
in *Helpers and Aides*:
Bath Workers
Servants and Other Domestic Laborers
in *Manufacturers and Miners*:
Power and Fuel Merchants

Brewers

Brewers make an alcohol beverage from starchy raw materials, such as cereals, which are steeped in water, boiled with hops, and fermented. Beer, the resulting product, has been a popular drink since ancient times. The earliest brewers were generally women, who made beer at home for local sale. These *alewives* operated in rural communities for thousands of years, up into modern times. The Egyptians believed that the god of agriculture—Osiris—had taught the art of brewing. They had many laws against those brewers who made under-strength beer. Commercial breweries also operated in both Babylon and Ur. In China and Japan brewers used millet, rather than the more common barley grain.

Beer became especially popular in northern Europe, where wine grapes did not grow well. Brewers there

Country people—many of them women known as alewives—made beer for thousands of years. (By W.H. Pyne, from Picturesque Views of Rural Occupations in Early Nineteenth-Century England)

worked closely with bakers, who offered them coarse by-product grains for use in their beer processing; often the same person was brewer and baker. Medieval monks—particularly the Trappists—greatly improved the brewing process. Although the British Domesday Book records 43 *cere visiarii* (breweries), most brewing was the product of cottage industry or domestic production. Many women both brewed and sold beer, which was subject to the landlord's inspection and taxation. As towns developed, many brewers both made and sold beer in city drinking establishments. Increasingly, beer became an essential ingredient in the northern European diet.

Large commercial breweries anticipated developments that took hold with the coming of the Industrial Revolution. Brewers used extensive and large-scale mechanization with relatively few laborers as early as the 17th century, while most industries before the 19th century were labor-intensive, using little machinery, if any. Brewers in major cities in England, Holland, and Germany were among the first capitalists, because of the large outlays, investments, and overheads that were a part of their business. Some of the more successful ones were even moneylenders who helped other industries develop.

Today large corporations own and operate most breweries. Worldwide, a handful of such conglomerates monopolize the industry and distribute their product to both national and international markets, made possible by rapid bulk transportation. But in some parts of the

In large breweries, workers sometimes waded hip-deep in the mixture that would become malt beer. (By Gustave Doré, from London: A Pilgrimage, *1872)*

world, such as Britain, beer is still brewed on a small scale, sometimes by the *publican* who sells it. Even in large-scale operations, the *brewmaster* who must assess the quality of the product at every stage, has considerable status, compared to the *factory workers* who handle the bulk of the operations in the brewing process.

For related occupations in this volume, *Restaurateurs and Innkeepers*, see the following:
  Bakers and Millers
  Innkeepers

For related occupations in other volumes of the series, see the following:
in *Financiers and Traders*:
  Bankers and Financiers
in *Helpers and Aides*:
  Servants and Other Domestic Laborers
in *Manufacturers and Miners*:
  Factory Workers

Butchers

The profession of killing animals for food is thousands of years old. Ever since prehistoric times, humans have hunted wild animals to supply themselves with nourishment and sustenance. As roaming bands of nomads began to raise animals in herds for ready meat supplies, societies became more stable. The Egyptians engaged mostly in bare subsistence herding, so that there was very little commercial activity concerning meat. In fact, meat was rarely eaten except for special feasts and at times of sacrifice. These occasions were hardly frequent or elaborate enough to support any kind of a profession to deal with meat preparation, a chore generally handled by royal *cooks* or *priests*.

There are some references to professional butchers in Babylonian times, however, and this may well have been where the occupation first emerged. At the same time and for the centuries that followed, butchery in India was considered an extremely "impure" trade, owing to the sacred esteem enjoyed under Hinduism by all living creatures, especially the cow. Some people, mostly non-Hindus, did practice the trade; but since the Hindus were a majority of the population and controlled the government, butchers were subjected to forms of ruinous taxation.

In ancient Greece many a pig farmer drove his herd to the Agora (the marketplace) each morning. There he enticed shoppers with calls of "buy sausage," although he would also sell whole pigs, alive or killed on the spot, as the customer desired. The Greeks generally ate very little meat though, especially the Athenians, who were extremely health-conscious and athletic. The beautifully conditioned, well-toned, healthy Greek athletes rarely touched meat.Their physicians and trainers believed (as some do today) that it caused digestive disorders, blocked natural energy, and overburdened the heart with heavy and wholly unnecessary fats. The Athenians were light eaters and vegetarians. They denounced the neighboring Boeotians as "flesh eaters," and regarded the habit as repulsive. When Greeks did eat meat, it was usually pork, very rarely beef.

The Romans, in contrast, were famous eaters of everything imaginable, and especially meat. Many butcher shops in the city marketplaces catered particularly to the wealthy, who considered it somewhat of a status symbol to eat meat. Pork, especially bacon and sausage, along with beef were their favorite meats. The mainstay of the butcher's livelihood though, was mutton (the meat of sheep) and cruder cuts of beef, since these were the most economic choices of the masses of the people who frequented his shop. The wise butcher also increased his income by offering goat to those too poor to afford the finer carcasses. Meat was extremely difficult to preserve in Roman times, yet it was usually too cumbersome and gory to slaughter animals at the time of a sale. Butchers used very crude methods of meat preservation, leading undoubtedly to many a disease.

Butchers were relied upon even more heavily in the Middle Ages. The great Mediterranean cultures of the Near East, Greece, and Rome had far more favorable climates for the growing of grains, vegetables, and fruits than did those of northern Europe. Since there were hardly any means of adequately preserving such foods for any appreciable period of time, however, people had to make do with what they could gather locally. For most Europeans this meant a diet heavy in meat, poultry, fish, and wild game. Under the feudal system of large castles and manors, the largest share of the burden of feeding the masses fell on the shoulders of the lord of the manor—the landlord.

Feudal peasants worked the fields and turned most of their harvest over to their lords, who actually owned the land on which the peasants lived and farmed. The peasants were also obliged to render military and civil services to the lord of the castle. In return, the lord offered the peasantry (as well as the nobility) personal

This butcher is preparing to slaughter the cow held by his assistant. (By Jost Amman, from The Book of Trades, *late 16th century)*

security, shelter, and sustenance. Food was often scarce in feudal kingdoms, however; and since commerce and transportation were virtually nonexistent, each lord had to provide his own in some way.

The typical method of feeding the masses was to stockpile foodstuffs until emergency situations arose, as they did periodically. Then the lord would invite his starving subjects into the courtyard or adjacent streets for a feast that would last until the allotted rations were consumed. Such feasts lasted for days and consisted of bread, meat, wine, and whatever else could be found. The people were so glad to finally have some food that they commonly used different forms of emetics—substances that induce vomiting of already eaten food so that more might be stuffed in. The Romans had done this frequently out of the sheer desire to enjoy as much food as they possibly could. Medieval peasants did likewise, a practice that thrived well into the 18th century. The peasantry typically induced vomiting with strange concoctions such as mustard and salted water. Gentlemen had finer tastes; they used emetics sweetened to a revolting degree.

Teams of butchers and cooks were commissioned or drafted by the lord to make such feasts successful. To be considered successful, a feast had to have an abundance of food and had to stretch out over a period of at least several days, preferably a week. Butchers finely chopped slaughtered game for such events and were also given the chore of obtaining and preparing any additional dishes that might further appease the throngs. Accordingly, they hunted down rats, dogs, cats, and even lame horses and other beasts of burden to serve upon the lordship's table. The job involved furious activity while it lasted, but there really was no concept of free commerce at the time; in any case, there was not enough livestock to be slaughtered to allow these butchers to develop any professional trade or service.

Most of the butchers who served the medieval world were wandering peddlers. They were underhanded and lowly creatures who occasionally even resorted to intercepting highway travelers and carving their cooked flesh to sell as "pork." Customers sometimes heard of such practices and were therefore wary of such items. But many were not about to probe the matter too deeply, when the price was fair and they had starving children at home. Human flesh vendors were particularly active in Central Europe—Poland, Transylvania, and several German principalities. The practice (or malpractice) may have had a considerable influence on the development of werewolf and vampire legends in that part of the world—legends that remain very much alive even today, although the business that gave them birth has been abandoned. Chinese butchers, too, were known to have sold a cheap "two-legged mutton" during severe famines in the 12th century.

As towns began to develop with the decline of the feudal age, there was a greater demand for butchers to supply townspeople with meat. Every medieval city had butcheries and butchers' guilds. Many guilds had regulations limiting or banning the slaughtering and purveying of dogs, cats, and horses. Most butchers did their slaughtering "on the hoof" at the time a sale or agreement was made; that ensured the customer of the freshness of his purchase. But one could never be sure of the quality of even fresh meat. Certainly many people

While some butchers are cutting apart carcasses, two others prepare to stun an animal before slaughter. (From Diderot's Encyclopedia, *late 18th century)*

were seriously diseased or poisoned by the meats purchased at butchers' shops, and a significant number of those died. Filthy butchers' shops and unclean handling procedures were part of the problem, as were the unsanitary conditions of town life.

Butcher-shop districts were typically the worst parts of town, and many municipal laws and guild regulations aimed at getting them cleaned up. The streets were strewn with blood and animal parts, which were "cleaned" only by free-roaming pigs and hard rains. By the 13th century a certain type of large black rat was so common that shoppers often had to swat them away in order to take their purchases in hand. The black rats were infested with disease-laden ticks and fleas that swarmed throughout open-air markets (as all shopping districts were). The rats were largely responsible for spreading the terrible plagues and epidemics of Europe. The worst was the Black Death in the 14th century, in which from one-third to one-half of the European population died. Rats were especially fond of the butchers' shops, passing on diseases to animals in the slaughterhouse whether the stock were dead or alive. The stench that rose from the shops was so abominable that just smelling it was commonly thought to cause disease. Prepared and cut meats hung openly on hooks and ropes, where dogs and cats could freely lick at them until they were wrapped for someone's dinner.

Municipal laws and royal decrees were constantly being devised to try to deal with the evils of the abhorrent trade in butchered meats, but few were effective. In 1369 the British king, Edward III, advised London municipal authorities of a "grievous complaint" he had received from townsmen living near the *shambles* (slaughterhouse) of St. Nicholas. It concerned:

> . . . the slaughtering of beasts in the said shambles, and the carrying of the entrails and offal of the said beasts through the streets, lanes and places aforesaid to the said banks of the river . . . where the same entrails and

offal are thrown into the water aforesaid . . . the droping
of the blood of such beasts between the said shambles and
the waterside aforesaid—the same running along the
midst of the said streets and lanes—grievous corruption
and filth have been generated . . . so that no one, by
reason of such corruption and filth, could hardly venture
to abide in his house there.

Despite the king's good intentions, nothing significant
was done to improve the situation. In Paris in 1419
"Charles by the Grace of God" actually ordered butchers
and *knackers* (people who bought disabled livestock and
sold the animals' meat and hides) to remove their filthy
shops to the outer fringes of the city limits:

We have commanded, and we command, so that the air
of our said city be not infected or corrupted by these
slaughterhouses and *knackers'* yards, and also that the
water of the river Seine be not corrupted nor infected by
the blood and other filth of the said beasts falling or
being thrown into the said river Seine, that all
slaughterhouses and knackers' yards establish
themselves outside our said city of Paris . . .

Despite complaints, the profession continued to
prosper, especially in serving the wealthy classes that
could afford the high-priced meats. And as if squalid
work and retail shops were not enough, butchers even
dabbled in doctoring the already putrid product.
"Blown-out" meat was a common trade trick (devised
without the modern benefit of hormonal injections) to
make the buyer believe that he was getting a larger piece
of meat than he actually was. In France, pork inspectors
known as *langueyeurs* had to be appointed to see that
butchers were not trying to sell ulcerated pigs' tongues,
an item believed to cause leprosy. In addition to all of this,
the towns themselves were so dirty and diseased that
roaming animals were infected either directly by eating
and drinking or indirectly through constant contact with
parasites of all sorts.

In Spain, as late as the 17th century, such a situation existed in no less a city than Madrid. People living in townhouses threw their garbage and waste carelessly into the middle of city streets, there being no garbage removal or sanitation services. Butchers did likewise, of course, adding further to the mess. The priest who would later become Pope Paul V described an unbelievable stench in the streets during a visit to Madrid in 1594. He explained part of its source: "Among other defects, the houses had no privies. Thus the inhabitants relieve themselves into chamberpots, which are emptied out of the window."

Gradually such "emptying" became restricted to certain times of the night—after 10:00 P.M. in the winter and after 11:00 P.M. in the summer. The throwing from balconies of "water, refuse, and other things" was conventionally preceded by the public warning of "Aqua va!" ("Beware water!") shouted into the streets below. But it eventually became illegal to empty chamber pots from anywhere other than the street level front door. While these rules helped a little, the disgusting slop that every sort of beast wallowed in for months before slaughter was certain to have telling results in the butchers' shops. There was a popular—and undoubtedly true—adage of the day to the effect that one ate and drank in the summer what he expelled in the winter.

Despite the squalor of towns in general and butchers' shops in particular, the trade thrived, especially with the wealthy classes of society. Part of the reason was that marketing itself became more popular as urban centers grew. Transportation was still poor, however, and preservation of meats was a continual problem for the butcher.

In China, butchers were kept busy by the heavy demand for what were thought to be extremely healthful delights, such as blood soup of any type, and heart, kidney, and lung soups, salads, and pastes. Street vendors in Kaifeng sold sheep shanks to restaurants and passersby.

The popularity of butchered items can be gleaned from an account of a banquet given in 1612 by the Duke of Mayenne as he sought the hand of the Infanta, Anne of Austria. Besides gargantuan provisions of poultry, each feast-day included one hundred hares, twenty-four sheep, two quarters of beef, twelve ox tongues, twelve hams, and three pigs.

Even travelers sought out butchers' services; often they bought raw meats or small game from hunters who set up makeshift butcheries on well-traveled highways. Once the traveler arrived at his evening's lodging, he could check into a room and take his meat provision from his coat pocket (such precious cargo could no nowhere else) and hand it over to the innkeeper. The innkeeper would butcher and cook it himself and return it to the guest, or he might turn the matter over to the house butcher. Many a traveler was certain that the meat he surrendered in such manner was not the same that he received when called to dinner, however. For that reason it became more common for travelers to seek out a commercial butcher in

With his assistant looking on, this butcher cuts up some meat for his customer. (By Gustave Doré, from London: A Pilgrimage, *1872)*

town and pay a fee for the same service, but with presumably more honest results.

In many cases roadside hunter-butchers acted outside of the law, since town guilds generally monopolized the trade. In Spain it was illegal for farmers to sell their own livestock, unless they had purchased a license to collect taxes on it. If they did, they were duly authorized as *tax-farmers*, but the influence of the butchers' guilds still made it unlawful for them to slaughter or package meat cuts for sale. Moonlighting butchers of all sorts managed to evade such laws by selling their goods deep in the forest or on Sundays, when the authorities were preoccupied. Even the *ratcatchers* employed by captains of seagoing vessels making voyages to the New World or elsewhere got a piece of the action. Due to the lack of meat preservatives at that time in history, meats packed for such trips went bad very quickly. Only a week or two into a journey of some months, the only meat available was dry, leathery, rancid, and fully diseased. Ratcatchers had the only reasonable access to fresh meat. Even though they were supposed to have kept the river pests out of the storage bins while the ship docked at harbor, it was always suprising how many had made their way aboard. Once the ship was on the open sea, ratcatchers set up shop butchering and sometimes even cooking "fresh" rats. The delicacy sold at an exorbitantly high price, so that the ratcatcher-butcher who accompanied Columbus on many of his voyages was said to have died a rich man. (Columbus might have been in the wrong business, judging from his lack of wealth at the time of his death.)

Most people did not use the services of butchers, even as the Industrial Revolution began. Well into the 19th century most butchers' shops received livestock strictly on the hoof, and they still hacked it up well in advance of sales. There was still no adequate method of meat preservation. And customers did not really know how long meat had been hanging on the hooks or decaying in wire or mesh "meat-safes" (the latter were commonly used right up to World War II to store smaller cuts of meat). All meat—smoked, sugared, or salted—was hung in the open air to drain and dry, thus being open to all kinds of disease-carrying parasites. Meat remained extremely expensive, so that only the well-to-do could afford it on a regular basis in any case. But the wealthiest people, especially the landed country aristocracy, preferred to do their own hunting for game or herding of livestock. They then had their own domestic cooks and butchers do the preparation for what they could count on as being fresh meat. Mrs. Hannaly Glasse's cookbook for domestic use, written in 1747, contained the famous instruction "First Catch your Hare . . ."

The development of better food preservation, notably the first refrigeration unit, patented in England in 1834, allowed longer storage life and less bacterial intrusion. The most significant factor in the modernization of the butchers' profession was the advent of the railroad and particularly the refrigerated boxcar. These developments allowed the long-distance shipping of already killed and sometimes partially cleaned livestock directly to butcheries. By the mid-19th century, most butchers had stopped receiving animals on the hoof and had pretty much abandoned the practice of seeking out their own animals to hack. This alleviated much of the infamous practice of grabbing lame horses, rats, and stable dogs, packaging them to disguise their origins, and offering them for sale as pork or "combination meats." But hard times could bring a reversion to old practices. A picture of a butcher's stall set up in the streets of Paris in 1870, when the city was under siege by the Germans, shows unskinned but dead and sometimes halved or beheaded rats, dogs, and cats proudly displayed on the street counter. Customers of all classes, including gentlemen, are pictured buying provisions at the little shop, its signs boldly advertising: *"Rats"* and *"Viande Canine et Feline."*

For the most part, butchers had cleaned up their trade considerably by the time of the great urbanization that accompanied the Industrial Revolution. In America, the vast and open plains were ideal places for raising cattle and hunting buffalo. Long cattle drives usually terminated at railroad stations in Midwestern urban centers such as St. Louis or Kansas City. From there livestock was shipped to the great slaughter and meatpacking houses in Chicago, New York, and elsewhere. The new urban and laboring classes of people demanded the services of the city butcher as well as the large meatpacking firms. Slaughterhouses in the Midwest became notorious for their foul handling practices, a situation that is still being constantly inspected. And the problem was not confined to America. A shambles in London's Smithfield market in 1845 was "an irregular space bounded by dirty houses and the ragged party walls of demolished habitations." It held as many as 4,000 oxen and 30,000 sheep, to say nothing of countless pigs and calves, all awaiting slaughter and subsequent shipment to butchers and restaurants. The butchers at these large factories must have been quite a sight. One observer noted how they were:

> . . . wading in blood and covered with it all over. Between them lay the skulls and bones, strewed about in wild confusion; the entrails, which were afterwards loaded upon waggons and carried off; and beyond . . . the unborn calves were lying, in a heap of perhaps thirty or forty; near which, boys standing up to their shoulders in blood, were engaged in stripping off the skin of the largest and most matured ones.

The vast increase in the numbers of butchers in most cities and the larger volume of meat being handled brought about stricter regulations concerning meat slaughtering, processing, packing, and preserving. But a great many practices were still overlooked, and the quality of the butchers' products was rarely questioned by municipal inspectors. Butchers found many ways to make side money beyond the selling of cut meats. Slaughterhouses sold just about every scrap available to butchers or manufacturers—even tripe, the rubbery lining of the animal's stomach. Meat by-products were used in the manufacture of glue and sausage. A plush slaughterhouse in Paris in 1890 was the scene of stately women of leisure purchasing medicinal glasses of blood from attending butchers. Watching these women sip from fine crystal wineglasses, people could only wish that they also could afford to partake of the supposed health beverage.

With meat arriving from great distances in refrigerated rail cars (as early as 1850, meat was brought to London butcheries from 500 miles away), butchers put more effort into customer relations and the cultivation and display of their art. Even in 1830 Boston butchers courted their high-class clientele by wearing fine suits, bow ties, and stately black top hats as they hacked meats to specification. In *Martin Chuzzlewit*, Charles Dickens eloquently describes the art of the butcher through the eyes of his fictitious characters, Tom and Ruth Pinch:

> To see the butcher slap the steak, before he laid it on the block, and gave his knife a sharpening, was to forget breakfast instantly. It was agreeable, too—it really was—to see him cut it off, so smooth and juicy. There was nothing savage in the act, although the knife was large and keen; it was a piece of art, high art; there was delicacy of touch, clearness of tone, skillful handling of the subject, fine shading. It was the triumph of mind over matter; quite. Perhaps the greenest cabbage-leaf ever grown in a garden was wrapped about this steak, before it was delivered over to Tom. But the butcher had a sentiment for his business, and knew how to refine upon it. When he saw Tom putting the cabbage-leaf into his pocket awkwardly, he begged to be allowed to do it for him; "for meat," he said with some emotion, "must be humoured, not drove."

The 20th century marked greater governmental control over the meat industry in general, and therefore over the activities of many professional butchers and over the final product to be marketed. One of the most eloquent portrayals of abuse in the industry came from the pen of Upton Sinclair, who wrote *The Jungle* in 1906. Set against a backdrop of the Chicago slaughter and meatpacking industry, the novel showed unsanitary horrifying working conditions that so revolted Americans that they virtually stopped buying canned meat altogether in the summer of 1906. By the end of that summer President Theodore Roosevelt had helped push through the country's first Meat Inspection Act aimed at making *embalmed beef* (as Sinclair called it) and all other packaged and butchered meats safer for human consumption. Similar legislation has followed throughout the world.

Today, butchers own shops in virtually every city, town, and hamlet in the world. They also work in large restaurants and hotel kitchens and in large general merchandise food markets and grocery stores. Many belong to large, powerful, and protective labor unions. Most of the procedures and techniques employed in the treatment of commercial meat are now controlled by legislation, which, in turn, is enforced by teams of civil and trade union inspectors. Despite all this, there is ever-increasing public questioning of the "approved" treatment and nutritional value of meat.

Commercially raised livestock are usually housed in very close and unhealthy quarters. Such conditions make the animals so prone to disease that large amounts of antibiotics are used routinely to prevent or counter it. In addition, animals are often raised on cheap, poor quality foodstuffs, which are compensated for by the liberal injection of bloating growth hormones. When people buy "fresh meat" from their butcher shop or supermarket, they are usually getting meat that includes chemical additives and sometimes artificial colorings and flavorings, and is usually "blown-out" and therefore highly fatty and gristly. Most commercially raised livestock can no longer roam and graze, so they usually have a much lower concentration of muscle and fiber and a much higher fat and cholesterol count. One wonders

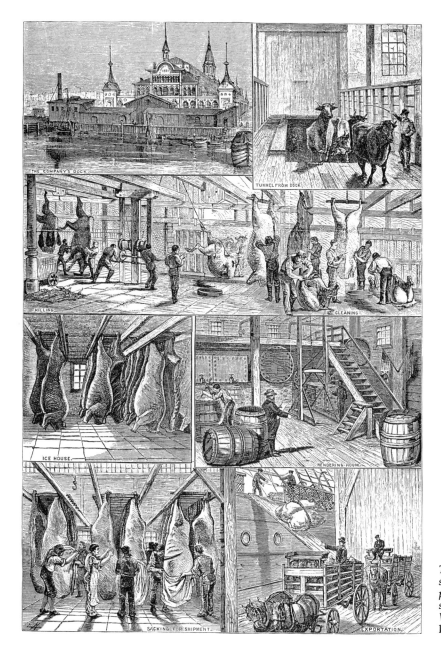

This cross section of a Manhattan slaughterhouse shows the whole process from arrival of animals to shipment of packaged meat. (By V.L. Kingsbury, Harper's Weekly, *July 7, 1877)*

how much better this product is than Sinclair's "embalmed beef." With the steadily rising costs of raising and therefore selling meat, and the increasing public questioning of its nutritional value, the future for professional butchers and their organizations of laborers may not be quite as rosy as their recent past and present.

For related occupations in this volume, *Restaurateurs and Innkeepers*, see the following:
   Cooks
   Innkeepers
   Poulterers

For related occupations in other volumes of the series, see the following:
in *Harvesters*:
   Farmers
   Hunters
in *Helpers and Aides*:
   Exterminators and Pest Controllers
   Sanitation Workers
in *Leaders and Lawyers*:
   Inspectors
in *Scholars and Priests*:
   Priests

Confectioners

Confectioners derived their special craft of making sweet pastries and candies from the *baker*. The earliest confectioners were bakers, who sold candy and cake along with bread. Even today, most bakeries also sell confectionery items as well as baked products. But the many strictly confectionery shops make and sell just candy or cake, and in modern times ice cream, as the confectioner's trade overlaps with that of the *dairy worker*.

Sugar was virtually unheard of in the ancient Western world, although it was a commonly used preservative in China and Japan. The Egyptians had very few confectionary items, and even honey was a rare treat. Fruits served the purpose in this department, and we know that figs were the typical treats packed carefully away in Egyptian tombs. The Romans also used fruits for sweeteners. Bakers and confectioners made cakes sweetened with fruits and honey, as well as fancy fruit pastries, which were quite a favorite at dinner parties. Confectioners found ingenious ways of preserving a sort of candied fruit that was in great demand and sold for a rather high price.

In the Middle Ages many a fine household retained a *pastry cook* as part of its kitchen staff, and in the cities, public confectioneries and pastry shops became quite popular. Professional confectioners sold a special sweet wafer in their shops that became a standard snack all over Europe. In China, confectioners sold sweets for centuries, and peddlers walked the streets, offering such treats as peanuts, candy, and pastries to men rushing on their way to and from their daily businesses.

Just as Europe's honey supplies were being rapidly depleted, making honey quite expensive, sugar began to be cultivated in the New World. The Spanish first harvested South American raw sugarcane in 1506. The Portuguese soon began using the available supply of native slaves for plantation sugar production, and by the middle of the 17th century the Dutch had joined in similar activities. Brazilian sugar became a hit with Europeans seeking an economical substitute for honey. By 1600 they were using it widely as a preservative for fruits, and a century later jams were found on the shelves of the finer confectionery shops. With sugar widely available, the confectioner's business began to soar and new types of treats began to find their way into confectionery shops, bakeries, inns, and general merchandise stores. Many confectioners did not retail their products, but only made them for wholesale distribution to retail establishments or to common peddlers who carried them into remote country areas.

Edward Kiddler was a well-known *pastry-master* of 18th-century London. He opened a school in the city "For the Use of his Scholars" and wrote a book with recipes for "Pastry and Cookery" to accompany the class. He was so successful in teaching the art of confection making that

Confectioners used a wide variety of molds in making many of their sweets. (From Diderot's Encyclopedia, *late 18th century)*

he soon found himself teaching classes every afternoon except Sunday, and even provided that "Ladies may be taught at their own Houses." Given the success of his school—one of the earliest cases of formal adult education—the schoolmaster was unlikely to have found the time to act again as a professional "Pastry-maker."

In the 1760's Mrs. Elizabeth Raffald operated a confectioner's shop alongside her cooked-meat establishment on Fennel Street in Manchester, England. Her specialty was "Bride and Christening Cakes," and in 1766 she offered published "thanks for the great encouragement she meets with" in the baking of such items. The passage continues: ". . . and those who are pleased to favour her with their commands, may depend on being served with such cakes as shall not be exceeded." When she moved to a larger shop in Exchange Alley in the Market Place, she widened the range of her confection items and apparently combined the meat and confectionary shops:

> Here can be seen a large assortment of fresh Confectionary goods, as good and as cheap as in London. There may be had Creams, Possets, Jellies, Flummery, Lemon Cheese Cakes, best boiled Tripe, and pickled Walnuts. Also Yorkshire Hams, Tongues, Brawn, Newcastle Salmon, Sturgeons, all sorts of pickles, and Ketchups of

many kinds. Coffee, Tea and Chocolate of the finest sorts, and the best portable soup for Travellers.

Apparently there was more than one way for a confectionery apprentice to earn a living and reputation. Frederick Nutt, for example, once worked at the reputable cake and pie shop of Negri and Witten at Berkeley Square. In 1789 he published a book—*The Complete Confectioner; or the Whole Art of Confectionery: Forming a Ready Assistant to All Genteel Families*—aimed at teaching his professional secrets. Domestic confectioners held enviable positions in noble English and French households, and only the best were sought, even if they had to be recruited from across the sea. In the early 19th century, the Duke of Buckingham retained a kitchen staff that included an English roasting-cook, a French chef, and an Italian confectioner.

Commercial confectionery shops competed strongly with bakeries, and it was often difficult to determine whether the proprietor was a confectioner or a baker. Bakers commonly sold funeral cakes in 19th-century England, yet one advertisement offers this: "Biscuits and Breads for Funerals, made and sold by M. Wylde, Confectioner, Runcorn." Professional distinctions aside, both bakers and confectioners were being roundly criticized by the 19th century for their negligent or even criminal productions of food items. An 1845 British report claimed

These confectioners are making the traditional sugarplums and sugarcoated almonds. (From Diderot's Encyclopedia, *late 18th century)*

that confectioners made and sold pretty rainbow-colored candies and chocolates, which were in great demand because of their visual as well as savory appeal. The problem was that the pretty rainbow effect was produced by the scandalous adulteration of the confectioner's not-so-good goodies with extremely poisonous copper and lead salts.

Confectioners continued to sell a wide array of sweets, either directly in their own shops or indirectly through wholesale markets, such as general stores, which were increasingly common by the late 19th and early 20th centuries. A major jam and preserves fad stormed Victorian England, and since then jams have been standard stock in general merchandise shops. Candies and sweets today are rarely made by artistic confectioners carefully stirring to perfection sweet concoctions in the back rooms of shop quarters. Most items that confectioners now sell and make are mass-produced with the aid of machines in large factories that are staffed by scores of unskilled laborers. Most such items are marketed wholesale to all-purpose food shops and markets. There is little room for the artistic confectioner in today's society, except in resorts or similar places where their products are a novelty. Nonetheless, sweets have never been in greater demand, and large manufacturers of them now reap greater profits than ever before.

For related occupations in this volume, *Restaurateurs and Innkeepers*, see the following:
Bakers
Cooks
Costermongers and Grocers
Dairy Operators
Restaurateurs

For related occupations in other volumes of the series, see the following:
in *Financiers and Traders*:
Merchants and Shopkeepers
in *Manufacturers and Miners*:
Factory Workers

Cooks

Cooks—those who prepare food specifically through heating it, and altering its actual chemical structure to varying degrees—have been around ever since prehistoric humans discovered how to make fire and apply it to food. But cooking as a profession apparently developed from the very early periods of history, when kings, wealthy nobles, and priests used slaves to staff their large kitchens and prepare their banquets. Cooks also accompanied royal armies while on campaign and even prepared sumptuous sacrificial meals for deities, sometimes on a daily basis (as was common in Mesopotamia) and sometimes only during ceremonial feasts.

In ancient Greece the cooks for royal and wealthy families were usually *slaves*, but for formal dinners with guests, hired experts were sought. A man would generally send a slave into the business district to cry out solicitations such as: "Who wants an engagement to cook a dinner?" Most searches ended with the hiring of Sicilian *metics* (foreigners living in Greece but enjoying no citizenship rights). They usually cooked on a free-lance basis, and several had such good reputations that they were eagerly sought and could demand very high rates of payment, especially for important dinners or feasts. Many such cooks groomed their sons to work as their apprentices and assistants, preparing them for the day when they would take over the entire enterprise on their own. Sicilian cooks were proud of their craft and often boasted that theirs was the king of all professions. After all, their sales pitch went, they had to be learned in astrology, that they might choose the proper seasonings; in geometry, that they might procure the most appropriate boiler and judge accurately its best setting; and in medicine, so that only healthful dishes would be prepared. The Sicilian cook was also a grumbler, constantly berating the *spit-boy* and others of his assistants who did not have his knowledge or skill.

As late as 174 B.C. there were no professional cooks in the Roman Republic. But by the time of Augustus, less than two centuries later, there were a great many grand masters who "can tell at first bite whether an oyster comes from Circeii, or the Lucerine rocks or clear from Britain; or at one glance to discover the native shore of a sea-urchin." In imperial Rome, eating became one of the favorite pastimes of the entire elite. Dinner parties were held at the home of hosts almost constantly, so that wealthy people rarely dined at home, unless they were acting as host to guests. Expert slave cooks were purchased or rented at extremely high cost to prepare lavish feasts for their masters on a regular basis. Excessive eating was the rage of the day, and emetics (substances taken to cause vomiting) were used as casually as aspirins are taken today. Seneca described the typical Roman gluttons— which most well-bred and successful men of rank were—as those who "vomit that they may eat, and eat that they may vomit." The most famous Roman glutton was Marcus Apicius, who committed suicide when his fortune had dwindled to a "mere" ten million sesterces (about $400,000). He claimed that such a pittance could never support his eating habits and that he would rather die than change them.

The first mass food producers were the manufacturers of a popular Roman sauce called *liquamen*. People used it liberally, and there were several manufacturers of the delicacy in Pompeii, Antipolis, and Leptis Magna. One jar had a label reading: "Best strained liquamen: prepared in the factory of Umbricus Agathopus." These factories, which undoubtedly employed both slave and family labor, did not survive the fall of the Roman Empire.

In the Middle Ages most professional cooks were still engaged by the households of royalty, the landed aristocracy, and the priesthood. Some cooks became owners and operators of cooked-meat shops, taverns, and other commercial eateries, choosing the occupation of *restaurateur*. Teams of professional cooks were employed by lords, who stored food reserves and offered periodic

*Oil makers, who crushed and pressed various fruits, seeds, **and** herbs, were small-time manufacturers. (By Jost Amman, from* The Book of Trades, *late 16th century)*

feasts to their starving subjects. These feasts, usually given during famines and droughts, demanded all the cooks that could be mustered, but the job was not easy. Tank-loads of stews had to be kept brewing for several days, until the provisions were finally used up. The half-starved peasants drank wine liberally and kept stuffing the food down until they could eat no more. They would then retire from the banquet just long enough to vomit what they had eaten, only to return with a fresh appetite. Leather-aproned cooks worked feverishly to keep the mobs at bay; if they worked too slowly, they risked their very lives, when confronted by angry gluttons who had seen hardly any food for months. This was no time for fine cookery. The cooks grabbed anything they could to swell the stew pots—insects, gutter rats, stray cats, lame horses. Most of the diners were so inebriated that they would never know the difference.

Cooking began to reach more artistic levels during the Renaissance. European courts, especially those of the French and Italians, prided themselves on their family cooks. French *chefs* became world renowned as the best cooks in the world, and the chefs of Italy's Medici courts of the 16th century were equally praised. There were also

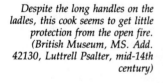

Despite the long handles on the ladles, this cook seems to get little protection from the open fire. (British Museum, MS. Add. 42130, Luttrell Psalter, mid-14th century)

more common cooks, such as those who worked professionally for large inns or taverns, or even for prosperous burghers. An early 16th-century woodblock print by Albrecht Dürer illustrates "The Cook and his Wife" as being a rather slovenly and overfed pair. The subjects are apparently "common" cooks, preparing food for the peasants, rather than household cooks.

John Murrell was one of the first professional free-lance cooks of the modern world. He earned a living not only by his cooking, which made him widely famous, but by teaching his craft in 17th-century London. He also sold cookbooks, in which he introduced the art of ornamental cookery. He even operated a shop from which he sold bread and gingerbread molds, and pots and pans, as well as his books. There were apparently many financial opportunities for renowned cooks beyond the art itself.

At about the same time, English court and noble society began to take a liking to continental cookery. French and Italian chefs were in great demand, particularly to be used as *head cooks*. Many British head cooks were sent to the Continent (especially to French courts) to learn the secrets of fine cookery. Their training, transportation, and boarding and lodging expenses were paid for by their masters. When they returned to England, they taught what they had learned to their eager *undercooks*. In Britain, at least, there was clearly a significant degree of patronage in the development of the cooking profession. Most household cooks remained with the same family for years. Robert May was employed as the chef of the Englefield family for nearly a quarter of the 17th century. The best opportunities for professionals remained in England for many years. The New World offered few opportunities for professional cooks, since the relatively few wealthy families often used Negro slaves to do the cooking and kitchen work.

Official chefs in Chinese courts were usually appointed to lifetime positions. Chinese household cooks were hard to come by, however, because there was such a great demand for them. Many completed formal training or apprenticeship only to pass up the household market to open their own restaurants instead. Some *restaurateurs* became so successful that they hired their own corps of chefs to rent out. Not all Chinese cooks were as amiable as they were skilled, however; frequent legislation was passed, designed to control their tempers and abusive language.

In the 18th century it became somewhat fashionable for British cooks to take advantage of their positions among royal and noble households. They began writing cookbooks that were as full of royal gossip and intrigue as recipes. One of the earliest such examples was *Royal Cookery: or, the Compleat Court-Cook* written in 1710 by Patrick Lambe, the "First Master Cook in the King's Kitchen." Other prestigious cooks wrote books imparting their special secret recipes and techniques to the general public—recipes that once had been reserved only for the families that hired the cook. Even public restaurants thereby gained access to distinctive food selections, and the professional cooks who worked for them thus gained access to the knowledge of even the royal cooks. John Nott, "Cook to his Grace the Duke of Bolton," published a cookbook in 1723 that was proudly advertised as being for "not only British Housewives, but Cooks, etc., in Taverns, Eating-Houses, and Publick Inns."

During this same period, there was an increase in nationalistic sentiments. This trend influenced the cooking profession, where national recipes and eating styles were beginning to supplant foreign and "exotic" ones. Even in England there were signs of dismay at the professed superiority of French foods and chefs to English foods and cooks. In 1747 Mrs. Hannah Glasse wrote a cookbook for British housewives, in which she stated flatly: "... so much is the folly of this Age, that they would rather be impos'd on by a French Booby, than give encouragement to a good English Cook!" Later she explained: "I have heard of a Cook that used six pounds of butter to fry twelve eggs; when every Body knows that Half a Pound is full enough—or more than need be used. But then it would not be French!"

By the end of the 18th century many more cooks in commercial eateries were establishing themselves as authorities in the profession. This was only possible, of course, because of the improving reputation of restaurants and inns. In 1783 John Farley, "principal cook at the London Tavern," made the inn a high spot in the city among notable gentlemen by dishing out sumptuous and original seven-course dinners. A few years later another cookbook was written by the "principal Cooks at the Crown & Anchor Tavern in the Strand." Even well-to-do persons were, by and large, beginning to give up their domestic cooks for economic reasons. As they did so, many cooks got jobs in fashionable restaurants, which in turn, drew more middle- and upper-class customers. Cooking, as a profession, began to take root in these commercial restaurants, although many wealthy families continued to retain domestic cooks, as they do even today. In those households where domestic cooks were kept on, economic factors began to make new demands on them. Mrs. Maria Rundell found an eager market for her book entitled: *A New System for Domestic Cookery: Framed Upon Principles of Economy, and Adapted to the Use of Private Families*. In it she suggested, among many other things, that:

> The cook should be charged to save every discarded scrap of boiled meat, ham, tongue, etc., however salt. It is easy to use only a part of that, and the rest of fresh water, and, by the addition of more vegetables, the bones of meat used by the family, the pieces of meat that come from the table and are left on the plates after eating, and rice, Scotch barley, or oatmeal, there will be come gallons of nutritious soup for the poor two or three times every week.

As foods became better preserved and more easily shipped during the 19th century, shopping became easier and many more people did their own cooking. Government standards slowly improved commercial food quality, so that shops and restaurants could be better trusted. In America, virtually all domestic cooking was done by housewives or slaves. Even Nathaniel Hawthorne, the well-to-do and notable author, did his own cooking during his wife's absence in 1844. He described the adventure briefly:

> The corned beef is exquisitely done, and as tender as a young lady's heart, all owing to my skilful cookery; for I consulted Sarah Hale's cookbook at every step, and precisely followed her directions. To say the truth, I look upon it as such a masterpiece in its way, that it seems irreverential to eat it.

By the 1880's it had become popular for cooking classes to be given by professionals to American housewives.

Outside of the industrialized parts of North America and Europe, cooks enjoyed little in the way of either social esteem or financial benefits. Most were employed in rough-and-ready restaurants, which had not felt the transforming touch of fashionable acceptance. Some were wanderers who worked roadside cookshops for travelers or went from town to town seeking temporary employment as cook for a festive or formal occasion. Others signed on as cooks for cattle drives, trading caravans, or hunting safaris. These patterns would continue in developed countries, even up to the present in some places.

But in the city-based cultures of North America and Europe, cooks enjoyed a much more elevated position. Perhaps no person better illustrates this than the famous 19th-century French chef. Alexis Soyer (1809-1858), of whom his biographer, Helen Morris, wrote:

> Among the less eminent Victorians was a man who wrote a book which sold a quarter of a million copies and who was caricatured in one of Thackeray's novels; who figured more often in the pages of *Punch* than many a Cabinet Minister; who was a dandy and a "card"; who saved the lives of thousands of soldiers and benefitted hundreds of thousands; who drew the breath of his being

from the French Romantics and who won the respect of Victorian England for his practical resourcefulness and powers of administration. He was only a cook, but he cooked for princes and paupers, and his booking had not a little to do with the growth of a great political party.

Clearly, Soyer was not "only a cook," but his widespread fame and political influence demonstrate the heights to which cooks could aspire. Florence Nightingale even brought him out to the Crimea to revamp the British Army's cooking techniques and diet.

Beyond the social status of chefs, the best ones gained considerable financial security, especially in England, where there were seemingly no limits to what a noble might pay to obtain a good chef. Soyer himself left France for England at an early age because of the rumors—quite true—of high pay there. Upon arrival he found many chefs living lives of luxury and sumptuous comfort. Many earned so much money that they were able to retire in full comfort after less than ten years of professional work. Soyer, too, was an instant success as a cook at several large London restaurants. At the age of 17, he already had 12 undercooks to supervise and teach. Of course, French chefs could always demand the highest salaries

Wherever large bodies of people were on the move, camp cooks followed. (By W.H. Pyne, from Picturesque Views of Rural Occupations in Early Nineteenth-Century England*)*

in England, but money was not always enough. Many French chefs complained bitterly about the British lack of fine taste and refinement. In one case, a chef named Felix left the service of the Duke of Wellington in an outrage, saying:

> I serve him a dinner which would make Ude or Francatelli burst with envy, and he says—nothing! I go out and leave him a dog's dinner half-dressed by an under-cookmaid, and he says—nothing! I cannot live in the same house with such a man—were he a hundred times as great a hero!

By the end of the 19th century most cooks in the world were working at public eating places. Domestic chefs were no longer common, except in Britain, where in the 1880's a great many upper- and middle-class households retained professional cooks. One cartoon of the day (by the social critic Sol Eyting) pictured a middle-class home in an uproar and the housewife in complete despair because the cook had quit her job. For the most part, though, cooks found their greatest and most abundant professional opportunities in restaurants and vacation retreats. Clubs were also popular in the early 20th century, as it became quite fashionable for the upper classes to dine regularly outside of the home. There was even a shortage of good cooks, thus improving the salary scales of those employed.

Some cooks continue to be employed in the domestic households of the well-to-do, but most work in restaurants, ranging from grimy little diners to plush nightclubs offering first-class entertainment along with lavish portions. Good cooks in elegant restaurants still demand extremely high pay and excellent benefits. This is especially true for those trained in the tradition of Georges-Auguste Escoffier, the famous turn-of-the-century chef who established the *chef bonnet*—called *gros bonnet* (literally, big hat)—as supreme in the kitchen, supported by other specialists, such as the *sauce chef* and the *pastry chef*. Such chefs are extremely com-

Throughout the years, people have delighted in demonstrations of culinary dexterity. (By J.N. Hyde, from Frank Leslie's, March 25, 1882)

petitive, continually testing their skills against those of their peers, and jealous of their standing in the world of food.

On the other hand the *short-order cook*, who often simply throws frozen, already prepared items into an oven for customers of fast-food convenience shops or diners, earns little more than do the waiters at such establishments—and has an attendant lack of status. Between these two extremes there are, of course, many professional levels. Many chefs are hired for their ability to cook national foods—Japanese, Chinese, French, Italian, Russian, Greek, or Indian, for example. Each type uses distinctive modes of cookery that correspond to the particular national flair for combining, seasoning, and decorating foods.

Today, as always, a good cook is in great demand and may expect to earn a substantial livelihood for his or her craft. Accomplished cooks may take years of formal schooling and apprenticeship (often served with father, mother, or other relative) to learn. A *quick cook* probably knows more about serving food without burning it than anything else. Such cooks have had little training and no formal schooling, and are easily replaced. Their salary and benefits are far less, and they are not social peers of the finer chefs. Men have traditionally dominated the cooking profession as a whole, but women have recently made their presence felt in the occupational ranks at all levels.

The last two centuries have also seen the rise of massive numbers of food preparers who make no pretense of being cooks, as the Industrial Revolution has thoroughly transformed the food industry. From the time of the Roman *liquamen*, occasionally enterprising individuals had packaged special preparations, such as mustards, for sales to others. But it was the development of canning, by Frenchman Nicholas Appert at the turn of the 18th century, that first allowed most foods to be preserved for a long time. The use of the tin (and later aluminum) can quickly followed, and soon canning factories were being set up around the world. The items canned were not only meat, fruit, and vegetables, and later fish, but also prepared foods of all kinds, such as stews and soups. On through the 19th and the 20th century, the canning of food expanded, allowing food to be brought from distant places such as Australia and Alaska to the prosperous countries bordering on the Atlantic.

In these mass-production operations, cooks play only a small role, usually working in *test kitchens*, perhaps along with *chemists, nutritionists*, and *dietitians*, experimenting with new recipes. Beyond these few specialists, the great majority of people staffing the food-production operations are *factory workers*, often unskilled people involved in increasingly mechanized production. Other unskilled or semiskilled laborers prepare food products for handling by the factories. These have been and often continue to be unpleasant jobs, whether the worker was a Chinese immigrant cleaning salmon in a California cannery, a Scotch *herring girl* gutting the widespread northern European fish, or an elderly woman plucking chickens in a smelly shed.

The great food-production factories of today are controlled by huge corporations, many of them household names such as Armour, Borden, and Swift, and form one of the largest industries in the world. The workers in the food industry clearly affect every social and economic level of society.

For related occupations in this volume, *Restaurateurs and Innkeepers*, see the following:
Bakers
Butchers
Confectioners
Innkeepers
Restaurateurs

For related occupations in other volumes of the series, see the following:
in *Healers* (forthcoming):
Nurses
in *Manufacturers and Miners*:
Factory Workers

Costermongers
and Grocers

Most of the foods that have been prepared for sale and sold directly to customers have been handled by *bakers, butchers, dairy operators, cooks*, and *restaurateurs*. But countless other food items have been sold by a wide variety of food vendors, called *costermongers* and later *grocers. Farmers* and *carters* regularly carried vegetables to ancient marketplaces, to sell at makeshift stands. Olive oil vendors were an exclusive lot in Greece and Rome, selling a highly prized item that was used as a body rub almost daily as well as a main ingredient in cooking. They drove tough bargains and usually came away with tidy profits. Fruit, onion, and garlic vendors were present at most marketplaces. Spice merchants were also important food sellers in most parts of the world.

Costermongers in Rome usually had to walk through the streets with trays of goods or squat near busy intersections. Many owned shops, which were nothing more than housefronts with counters on a main street; sometimes a whole street-level room was used for the family business. Living quarters in such places were usually dark and insufficient for raising a family. It was considered quite an insult to declare that someone was "born over a shop." Although street fountains provided public water in many places, vendors delivered water to the door for a fee, and some specialized in selling boiled water for cooking. Some general food merchants also sold fruit, vegetables, olives, and even some Eastern spices. Vendors usually yelled—or had a slave yell for them—into the marketplace to advertise their bargain prices or new stocks of fresh items. Many hucksters made a practice of blocking city streets to intimidate passersby into buying their goods. They caused considerable confusion and were always being chased by the emperor's civil soldiery. Food vendors sold most of their products to poor or laboring-class people. Gentlemen would rarely buy products from the marketplace, much preferring to have their own servants grow and prepare their food.

Merchants of Eastern spices had a thriving trade during the Middle Ages. Many European middlemen paid top prices to obtain the greatly desired items that came from China and India. In China, street vendors sold bite-sized portions of practically anything to those who rushed down the streets. Women sold salted vegetables and rice, and young boys carted peanuts, candy, pastries, soft drinks, and teas. Vendors even worked the all-night eateries, where they pushed herbs and dried fruits on customers sitting inside the restaurants. Sometimes they simply handed them out and then tried to collect their costs.

In Europe, traveling peddlers carried spices, trinkets—and gossip. Medieval food retailers could

*Costermongers rode through towns
and villages selling all manner of
fruits and vegetables. (From* Frank
Leslie's Popular Monthly
Magazine, *19th century)*

purchase dairy and produce items from farmers only at
set Friday and Saturday market fairs. Buying on con-
signment or by prearrangement was strictly prohibited,
to keep anyone from hoarding or black-marketing food
supplies in a time when starvation and massive food

shortages were a way of life. Offenders could be publicly executed. General food merchandisers also operated in some of the larger medieval cities. Sometimes referred to as *spice-grocers*, they stocked vinegar, oils, salt, pepper, sugar, honey, and even cooking utensils (which they also often repaired). *Greengrocers* sometimes allied themselves in guilds with *pharmacists*, with whom they shared an interest in herbs.

Throughout the centuries, roaming armies were frequently followed by teams of *canteen girls*, who sold drinks of all sorts, including water. *Tea merchants* made wild claims of healing and euphoria for their exotic Eastern products, which began to reach European markets in the 17th century. *Coffee merchants* also began to gain some popularity at that time. Ice and snow became important means of food preservation, and their merchants and vendors reaped hearty profits. In Spain, snow from the mountains was stored during the winter in *snow pits* for use in the summer. Many *puestos* (centers of sale) were set up by municipal governments, who tried to monopolize the prosperous trade themselves while they fixed both wholesale and retail prices.

In the 17th century Parisian costermongers displayed their goods on the filthy streets upon which they sat. In America at the same time only 20 percent of the populace lived in urban centers. Of the countryside, especially in the South, it was said that "the best of trade that can be driven is only a sort of Scotch peddling." By the end of the 18th century general food stores and country markets were becoming more commonplace in both Europe and America. General food merchants sold much more than food, however; they also stocked books, candles, hunting supplies, and anything else that might be popular. Most grocers bought food wholesale and in bulk and then packaged it themselves for retail sales. One caricature of the time gives us an idea of what grocers sold, for above the shop door was a sign that said: "Grocery, Sweetmeats, Hams, Tongues, Starch, Plumbs, Figs, Vermicelli, Tripe, Barley, Pickles, Mustard, Soap,

Some grocers set up permanent shops where they stored a variety of goods for sale. (From Picturesque Palestine, *19th century)*

Puddings & Sold here by Peter Figg." Many individual costermongers (the name originally meant *apple sellers*) still roamed the city streets and the countryside selling fruits, vegetables, eggs, fish (though these were usually sold by specialist *fishmongers*), and other such items. Many of these vendors, especially in the cities, were women.

The Industrial Revolution ushered in whole new concepts in food marketing. Large urban populations became increasingly dependent on food retailers, particularly general merchandisers. Better preservation of food and the mechanization of its packaging and production permitted its mass distribution to urban dwellers. Governments began regulating the processing, preservation, and adulteration of foodstuffs, so that grocers were increasingly able to gain the public trust. One of the first great supermarket chains was born in the 1870's in New York with the establishment of Hartford's Great American Tea Company, later named the Great Atlantic and Pacific Tea Company—shortened to A & P. Independent grocers increasingly gave way to large corporations, which ran chains of stores.

Ice vendors had a thriving business for the second half of the 19th century, and many a tale was told about the *iceman* who made deliveries. Huge chunks of natural ice were brought from Scotland and elsewhere for ready markets—restaurants, grocery stores, hotels, and private households. Some enterprising Yankee traders even sent shiploads of ice around Cape Horn to Panama City and across the ocean to Asia. But by 1900, with the arrival of mechanized refrigeration, ice vendors faced a drastically shrunken market for their food-preserving commodity, except in undeveloped tropical lands. Refrigerated ships were soon transporting fresh food all over the world, thus increasing the potential for the mass supermarket concept.

There are still food sellers of all sorts, who specialize in vending specific foodstuffs. One of the largest of the specialty grocers is the health food merchant, who has in recent years attempted to undercut the business of the supermarkets by selling more wholesome and less processed or adulterated foods. And street vendors still push carts or drive wagons or trucks through city streets selling every kind of edible treat to throngs of busy pedestrians.

For related occupations in this volume, *Restaurateurs and Innkeepers*, see the following:
- Bakers
- Brewers
- Butchers
- Confectioners
- Cooks
- Dairy Operators

Fishmongers
Restaurateurs

For related occupations in other volumes of the series, see
the following:
in *Financiers and Traders*:
    Merchants and Shopkeepers
in *Harvesters*:
    Farmers
    Hunters
in *Healers* (forthcoming):
    Pharmacists
in *Manufacturers and Miners*:
    Factory Workers

Dairy Operators

Milk, butter, and cheese—the main dairy items—were rarely used commercially before modern times. This may well be attributed to the poor methods of preservation available to prolong the life of such highly perishable items. The ancient peoples of Egypt, Greece, and Rome rarely drank milk, preferring instead beer and wine. The Greeks and Romans thought it extremely crude to use butter—essentially the fat skimmed off milk. They preferred, instead, to season their bread with olive oil, a far lighter substance to digest.

The peoples of the Far East agreed; they used dairy products only on very rare occasions. The peoples east and south of the Mediterranean made something of a virtue of their climate's effect on milk products: they developed yogurt, a staple food made from soured milk.

Yogurt was generally made for home use, however, and spawned no separate industries.

Dairy products were more popular in northern Europe, where the cooler climate allowed milk a slightly longer unspoiled life. There cheeses (known since ancient Egypt) were popular, and olives for oil were a rare commodity. Even so, the providing of milk and the making of cheese and butter were mostly family affairs throughout the Middle Ages, and even beyond. The exception was in the cities, where residents were too crowded together for each to keep a family cow. Nearby farmers would generally cart fresh milk into the town early each morning.

Later, as cities grew larger, *cow keepers* moved into the towns, putting their cattle out to graze in one of the many city parks or fields. Cow keepers would sometimes sell their milk directly to consumers, but more often they would distribute their product to various *milk sellers*, who in turn would have *milk carriers* peddle the liquid through the streets. This pattern continued and expanded through the Renaissance and into modern times, growing somewhat more elaborate as the cities grew larger.

Gradually a whole network of distributors came to be involved, as was found in 18th-century London, for example. Early in the morning, the milk seller would pick up his share from one of many cow keepers in London, taking the milk back to the cellar that served as the base of the business. Each milk seller had a territory known as a *milk walk*, much like a modern newspaper route. Through the series of streets that made up the milk walk, the milk seller—or, more likely, a servant or young female apprentice—would send up a cry, announcing his or her presence. The amount bought was marked in chalk on the customer's doorpost; the milk seller later tallied up the *milk score*. Milk sellers in 18th-century London had very low status; many of them were Irish, this being one of the few occupations open to them, as well as one that required only a small investment to buy the milk walk.

Milk girls were often dressed to appeal to male customers. (By T.L. Busby, from Costume of the Lower Orders, *1835)*

The *milkmaids* who did the actual street selling—and often the milking as well—were often even more unfortunate, since many of them were virtual slaves. In theory, the milkmaids were apprenticed, but in fact they had little prospect of gaining any skills to use after their apprenticeship was up.

The dairy trade was none too appealing in other ways as well. Milk was routinely sold as fresh, when in fact it had sat for a day at the cow keeper's until the cream rose and could be skimmed off. Not content with skimming the milk, the dairy operators then watered it down. Even that might not be so bad, but, as a late 18th-century report noted:

. . . the retailers are not even careful to use clean water. Some of them have even been seen to dip their pails in a common horse trough.

Nor did the people in the dairy trade have a very high opinion of each other. The same report also noted:

A cowkeeper informed me that retail milk dealers are for the most part the refuse of other employments, possessing neither character, decency, manners nor cleanliness. No delicate person could possibly drink the milk were they fully acquainted with the filthy habits of these dealers in it.

In the 19th century, technology was responsible for rapid growth in the sale of dairy products. In earlier centuries farmers and homesteaders in North America and Europe had increased their domestic production and use of dairy products, but it was the beginning of refrigeration and railroad transportation that really allowed the dairy industry to boom. Refrigeration—first used commercially in the 1830's—allowed milk, butter, and cheese to be stored and preserved beyond a few hours. Even so, the milk especially had to reach its market quickly, for refrigeration could only preserve milk for a few days, before it would begin to sour and curd—to say nothing of the rapid bacterial growth that brewed within. At the same time, new industrial urban centers increasingly separated country life from city life—in this case, food markets from food sources and suppliers.

To deal with this problem many dairy operators continued to follow the old pattern: they brought their cows to city greens, where they milked the animals and sold the beverage to passersby. Undercutting this business in the United States was the surprising number of urban residents who brought their own cows to the city, for domestic use and maybe a little extra income. The situation got so out of hand that individuals eventually had to petition municipal authorities for the privilege of keeping a cow in city parks and grounds. Josiah A. Jennings, for example, was granted a "License for one cow to go upon the Common for the year of 1829" in the city of Boston. Such licensing procedures made it increasingly difficult for dairy businesses to operate in cities, and by 1850 most serious dairy operators had moved beyond the city limits. Colonel Albert J. Pickett, who owned 20 cows just outside of Montgomery, Alabama, delivered nearly 100 quarts of milk per day to the city.

Dairy operators in North America were as unscrupulous as those in Europe. The watering down of milk was so common that one New York dairyman openly boasted that he "always accommodated his customers as to the price" of his milk. He did so by inquiring how much money each customer wished to spend on milk, and then mixed it with the right amount of water to bring the price in line with the offer. Another dairy operator passed his water through a sieve filled with cornmeal to give it a more milky look, so that it would not be so conspicuous when mixed with the milk—skimmed, of course. An investigation of Boston dairy dealers in 1857-1858 turned up only one case of pure and unadulterated milk being sold to the public. A Cincinnati milk dealer was once asked: "Do all dealers do it?" His answer: "No, the best milk dealers never put water in the milk, but rather put milk into water."

Although the railroad permitted faster transportation of dairy goods from farm to city, it did not really revolutionize the industry until mechanically refrigerated box cars were put into use in the 1860's. Before that time, most dairy operators continued to keep their cows on village greens or in the sheds standing next to the *cow keeper* shops. Cow keepers sold a wide variety of dairy products from their shops, sending out *milkmen* or *milk boys* on deliveries, usually to nearby restaurants and inns, and sometimes to individual homes. Since the milk, carried in open cans, became filled with insects (and, unknown at the time, thousands of microscopic bacteria) and turned cool in transit all over town, milkmen were instructed to

In turn-of-the-century Cuba, milk was still sold on the street direct from the cow. (From The New America and the Far East, *by G. Waldo Browne, 1901)*

skim off the insects and loose dirt, and to mix hot water with the product before each actual delivery. In this way the buyer was led to believe he was receiving clean milk that was still "warm from the cow."

Even worse were the dairy workers who kept their cows in distillery stables. Distilleries and breweries sold a by-product of the fermentation process (the process of making alcohol) for cow feed. This swill was cheap but nutritionally deplorable. The milk of cows fed purely on such a diet—as many were—was usually laden with bacteria. It became common for distilleries to rent out stable space to dairy operators, with the daily feeding of cows as part of the rental agreement. These cows, which were unexercised and fed a poor liquid diet, were highly prone to disease. One such distillery in New York housed 2,000 cows for dairy operators. A New York City newspaper account in 1838 lodged the following complaint concerning the distillery grains and swill used for feed:

These grains are corrupt and unhealthy; so much so, that they consume the flesh around the cow's teeth, also rotting the teeth, so that all these cows, becoming sickly in one year, are sent to the market to serve the people as a miserable substitute for beef, and 18,000 new and healthy cows are substituted in their place in one year to share the fate of their predecessors. So poisonous is their milk, that out of 100 children fed with it, 49 die yearly.

A considerable portion of the "distillery milk" was also whitened with plaster of Paris or chalk.

Cheese and butter were less important than milk commercially. They were usually made at home by women who labored feverishly at churning for several monotonous hours a day. The products were then marketed by street and country peddlers. As cheesemaking became more highly regarded as an art, some farmers began buying milk curd from other farmers and setting up small cheese and butter factories. In the United States, New York State and Ohio's Western Reserve became early centers of this industry. In the middle of the 19th century some dairy operators began making ice cream, a delicacy that soon became an extremely popular item.

This is the cheese-making process, Auvergne-style. (From Diderot's Encyclopedia, *late 18th century)*

After the refrigerated rail cars made dairy products more marketable, canning, chilling, and freezing arrived on the industrial scene to further improve prospects for the industry. In the 20th century, dairy operators have been busier than ever, supplying a receptive public with butter, milk, and cheese. The quality of dairy products has been improved dramatically through mechanization and processing techniques such as pasteurization and homogenization. Pasteurization (named for Louis Pasteur, who developed the process) involves heating and then rapid cooling to kill undesirable bacteria and other such organisms in the milk. Homogenization is a process that makes all the particles in the milk of roughly the same size, so the cream does not rise to the top, as in unhomogenized milk. Skim milk is milk from which the cream has been skimmed off.

Dairy operators made regular door-to-door deliveries in many Western nations for several decades before the development of neighborhood stores and large central groceries; in some areas they continue to do so to this day. They even sold their goods through street-side vending machines.

Today, dairy products are carefully controlled for quality and handling, and dairy operators find a more receptive and trusting public than ever before. But cows are still generally kept in crowded stalls, are under-exercised, sometimes undernourished, and often disease-prone because of dirty and unhealthy conditions. Rather than rectify this situation at its source, most commercial dairies feed cows regular doses of antibiotics such as penicillin to insure that diseases do not erupt severely enough to render their milk unusable; drugs are even fed to cows to stimulate lactation (milk production).

There is a small class of "certified raw milk" and "organic" dairy farmers, who are much more careful to avoid disease-potential conditions. They feed, exercise, and care for their animals better, and do not treat them with chemical drugs or antibiotics. Because they are so careful to raise healthy cows, some are able to bypass the pasteurization process, which detracts somewhat from the milk's natural nutritional value.

Small-scale dairy operators are rare today. Far more common are massive, mechanized plants, to which large milk trucks daily carry the milk produced by hundreds of dairy farms for many miles around. The processing of milk and the making of other dairy products, such as cheese, butter, and ice cream, are largely a mechanical process, with only a few specialists making the crucial decisions of timing and proportion. And the milkman and the milkmaid have been replaced by truck drivers delivering shipments of milk in containers to grocery stores and supermarkets.

For related occupations in this volume, *Restaurateurs and Innkeepers*, see the following:
Brewers
Confectioners
Cooks
Costermongers and Grocers
Distillers
Restaurateurs

For related occupations in other volumes of the series, see the following:
in *Financiers and Traders*:
Merchants and Traders
in *Harvesters*:
Farmers

Distillers

Distillers are able to make a drink that is higher in alcoholic content than either wine or beer. They do this through a process of boiling a fermented product and then recondensing the vapor into a liquid with greater alcoholic strength than the original. Many foods have been used by distillers as the base for this process; the most common one today is malted barley. *Stills* are used to contain the vaporization and recondensation that produce the various spirits.

As early as 800 B.C. the Chinese distilled rice beer, and in the East Indies *arrack* (a sugarcane and rice product) was distilled. Basic distillation techniques were developed in the Mediterranean region, reportedly by Mary the Jewess, who worked at the School at Alexandria, in the first centuries of the Christian era. But

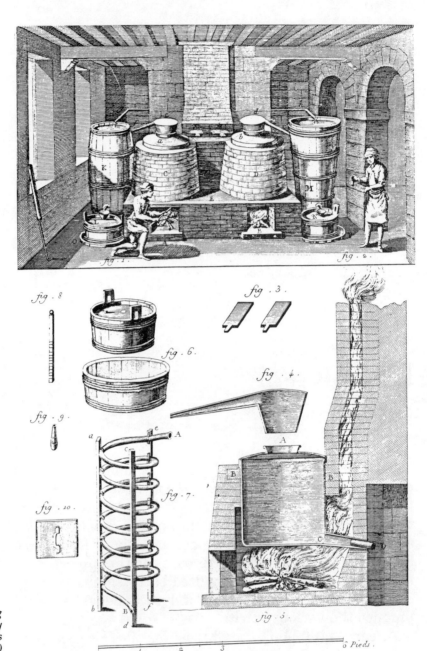

Distillers produced spirits using processes developed by the early alchemists. (From Diderot's Encyclopedia, *late 18th century)*

the popular commercial production and marketing of distilled products do not seem to have begun until the eighth century A.D. At that time some Moslems (who also made perfumes through distillation) were selling large amounts of distilled wine in the Near East and in Moslem Spain. From there the product found its way throughout the Western world. In Asia, cows' milk was the base used by commercial distillers, and elsewhere honey, oats, grapes, and malted barley were common.

By the end of the 13th century more efficient stills had been devised in Europe, and many more professionals found profit in the liquor trade. By the 17th century business was so good in many countries that governments had begun placing rigid controls on the industry. Distillers were a unique lot in the British colonies in North America, where they operated large-scale smuggling operations to evade British taxes and restrictions on their lucrative rum trade. Rum was an integral part of a major trade "triangle" that also involved African slaves and molasses (the latter being the base for rum fermentation). These dealings made the rowdy merchants of Newport, Rhode Island, famous in American Colonial history.

Even after the Colonies rebelled from England, distillers remained a powerful force. George Washington's administration—the first one in the United States' history—faced an attempted secession known as the Whiskey Rebellion, when a group of Western distillers fought Hamilton's excise tax on whiskey. The liquor was such a popular item in America that it was widely used as currency in place of gold, silver, and bank notes. The distillers convinced many Westerners that the whiskey tax indicated Washington's unfair bias toward protecting the Eastern economy at the expense of the West. Violence erupted in western Pennsylvania, where distillers even led a movement to create a local army. The new government quickly crushed the rebellion.

By the 19th century the sale of distilled liquors and spirits was a tremendous business that represented huge revenues for countries such as France, Britain, Russia, and the United States. Governments created rigid controls on the production and sale of liquor, widely considered a social evil. Like so many other social evils, liquor brought in great sums of money for both dealers—

distillers and merchants—and the governments that "controlled" them. Many distillers increased their profits considerably by selling their crude by-product swill to *cow* and *pig keepers* to feed their animals; city distillers even rented out stalls (including meals) for the keeping of dairy cows.

At about the same time that liquor production became a big business, many temperance groups, including the powerful Anti-Saloon League, made America a battleground for the issue of the legality of the selling and drinking of what some people regarded as "evil" spirits. Liquor distilling and sales were legally prohibited between 1919 and 1933 in the United States. This wild period, known as the Prohibition era, saw the unleashing of rampant mob activity centered on the illegal distillation and distribution of liquor. Violence and crime became so widespread that the government finally decided to legalize alcoholic beverages again, so that liquor would be sold by legitimate businessmen operating taxable distilleries instead of by underground crooks controlling a corrupt black market.

Today, large corporate distilleries with huge mechanized factories—each of which employs only one or a few experts in the distillation process—form one of the

These workers are bottling peach brandy from a still. (From Harper's New Monthly Magazine, *19th century)*

world's most profitable industries. In some places, such as Scotland, distillers—large and small—make a very substantial contribution to the economy. But some individual distillers continue to operate in secret, most notably in the Appalachian Mountains, where *moonshiners*—so called because many operate in the dead of night—carry the principles of the Whiskey Rebellion into modern times. On the opposing side are the government inspectors, who seek to find and tax the illegal stills, providing revenue for the government; as a result, they are popularly known as *revenuers*. The still-popular folk song, *Copper Kettle*, tells how moonshiners work:

> Get you a copper kettle,
> Get you a copper coil,
> Cover with new made corn mash,
> And never more you will toil.

The distillers who "watch them jugs a-fillin' in the pale moonlight" also have not forgotten the history of their old battle with the revenuers, noting that "we ain't paid no whiskey tax since 1792."

For related occupations in this volume, *Restaurateurs and Innkeepers*, see the following:
Dairy Operators
Innkeepers
Restaurateurs
Winemakers

For related occupations in other volumes of the series, see the following:
in *Healers*:
Pharmacists
in *Leaders and Lawyers*:
Inspectors
in *Scholars and Priests*:
Monks and Nuns
in *Scientists and Technologists*:
Alchemists
Chemists

Fishmongers

Fish was a regular dietary item in ancient times. In the
Greek marketplace, the *fishmonger* was an insolent but
highly respected professional. He rang a bell to announce
the arrival of fresh fish from one of the harbor boats. He
intimidated his customers and berated them loudly for
trying to talk down the price of his product. In Rome
many rich men raised their own fish in artificial ponds,
but commoners were frequent customers of the street
fishmongers.

In the Middle Ages fishmongers often sold fish that
had been taken from highly polluted rivers, which served
as garbage dumping grounds for rows of butcheries and
stables. Fishmongers' guilds in Venice forced all fish to
be hauled to the "tall pole" in the fish markets of San
Marco and the Rialto. There they were valued and taxed,

and fishmongers' stalls were inspected so that stale fish could not be sold. But fishmongers throughout the world regularly sold polluted and stale fish. Some would douse the fish with pig's blood to make it look more appealing. Freshening fish with water was an illegal act, but Italian *fishfags* were known for centuries to contrive to do so through a trick of the trade. One fishfag would knock down another in a contrived fight; bystanders would douse the victim—and coincidentally his fish, too—with water, thus freshening them both up a bit.

Fishmongers preserved their goods crudely by salting techniques, but in 1599 a complaint in Madrid stated that "on Friday as the fish-carts go to market, the stench is such that one has to close the windows." Friday was a big day for fishmongers throughout the Roman Catholic world, for every Friday church members were supposed to abstain from the eating of meat, but were allowed to eat fish instead. Considering the quality of the fish, they might have done well to eat only bread. In the late 18th century oyster-selling became a big fad in London and kept fishmongers busy, until the pollution of local waters forced the business to seek imports. These were so expensive that they drastically reduced the market.

Like many other occupations, fishmongering often ran in the family. The song celebrating Dublin's Molly Malone, for example, notes that: "She was a fishmonger, and sure 'twas no wonder,/For so were her father and mother before." In many such operations, one or two family members would run the main stall at the wharf or general marketplace. Others, especially children and servants, would hawk fish throughout the town, like Molly Malone, who "rolled her wheelbarrow through streets broad and narrow, Crying 'Cockles, and Mussels, Alive, Alive-O!'"

Today fishmongers operate shops in every city in the world and in many smaller towns. They have better methods of preserving their fish for longer periods of time, especially since the advent of refrigeration in the 1860's, but still rely essentially on their ability to offer

Billingsgate in early morning was filled with fishmongers hawking their fresh—and sometimes not-so-fresh—fish to customers. (By Gustave Doré, from London: A Pilgrimage, *1872)*

their customers a fresh product. Many fish are frozen and pre-prepared in large packaging firms, and are then distributed to supermarkets on a wholesale basis. But even in modern times, any port with fishing fleets has makeshift or semipermanent fish markets where fishmongers sell their products to all comers.

For related occupations in this volume, *Restaurateurs and Innkeepers*, see the following:

At the Fulton Fish Market, customers could buy fish from all over the East Coast of North America. (By Stanley Fox, from Harper's Weekly, April 3, 1869)

Butchers
Cooks
Costermongers and Grocers
Restaurateurs

For related occupations in other volumes of the series, see the following:
in *Financiers and Traders*:
    Merchants and Shopkeepers
in *Harvesters*:
    Fishers
in *Manufacturers and Miners*:
    Factory Workers

Innkeepers

In modern days, *tavern keepers* are typically thought of as the operators of establishments where alcoholic beverages are sold and consumed on the premises. Historically, though, taverns, inns, and saloons generally offered lodging as well as food and drink. Tavern keepers have apparently been in business since ancient times. An Egyptian papyrus dating back to about 1500 B.C. exhorts citizens: "Do not get drunk in the taverns."

In ancient Babylonia *innkeepers* held a status roughly equal to that of *diviners* and *physicians*. They were usually men of fairly adequate means and were even known to extend credit for beer sales to individual consumers. Often they were the chief *money lenders* in town. Besides offering lodgings and beer to travelers, they also arranged and catered large social gatherings and festive occasions.

In India innkeepers were a rough sort who had to double as *bouncers* when fights broke out among boarders, as they often did. Tavern keepers were sometimes forced to fly flags at the entrance to their establishments to indicate the poor quality of their rooms, drinks, or service. Indian innkeepers were made legally responsible for the property of their patrons, presumably because most petty thievery was done by the innkeeper himself while he was "cleaning" the rooms. Accordingly, he had to pay a prescribed indemnity to anyone robbed while staying in his inn.

Greek innkeepers were considered among the lowest of all citizens, since they not only served a clientele consisting mainly of drunks, thieves, and cutthroats, but also because they commonly harbored fugitives and runaway slaves for a fee. Roman innkeepers had to confine their sordid establishments to areas outside of the city gates. They offered mean lodging and questionable food to *teamsters* (drivers of teams of draft animals) and highway *robbers*. Gentry and people of class and self-respect preferred staying in private homes, sometimes as friends but other times as paying guests, or even camping by the side of the road. Most inns (*tabernae*) also housed horses, oxen, and other animals that were traveling with their masters.

Proxenus, keeper of the Inn of Hercules at the entrance of the Appian Way, was a typical member of his profession. He was from the Eastern Roman Empire, either Greece or the Near East. His inn was on the smaller side, but it had a large drive-in entrance for wagons to pass through. He lived in one of his own rooms near the stables, as most rooms were. There were only a few large rooms, and guests often had to share a bed with other guests and a host of bedbugs. The rooms were dirty but rates were cheap. Many a visitor left curses for the innkeeper scrawled upon the bedchamber walls; few people had anything good to say about Proxenus or others in his profession.

Innkeepers had a difficult time maintaining any

steady business during the Middle Ages. Petty warfare was constant and travel unprotected and extremely dangerous. For many centuries, most travelers in Europe stayed at monastery hospices, designed to shelter traveling pilgrims as well as the sick.

Travelers fared somewhat better in Asia, where many central governments, in China, India, and elsewhere, established *khans* or *caravanserais* specifically to serve the needs of traveling *merchants*. The caravanserais had rooms for the travelers, storage space for their goods, and enclosed yards for their pack animals. Operators of these establishments were sometimes private entrepreneurs (independent business owners), but frequently were employed by charities or the governments themselves. Often they were responsible for the safety of their charges. They usually gathered up all weapons at night, made a list of all the overnight guests, and locked everyone in at night. In the morning, they would check to see that every guest was accounted for; in some cases, they were even required to send the list on by messenger to the next caravanserai, as a method of ensuring that no one was lost on the way without the government knowing about it.

In Europe, as towns gradually developed and money became the standard medium of exchange, innkeepers again established businesses. Stronger central governments provided somewhat better protection for travelers, who cautiously took to the highways.

Many European inns of the early Modern Age had no beds at all, but only loose straw spread out on the floor or haylofts. Innkeepers commonly received visitors and cooked the raw-meat portions that the travelers had carried with them for days on the road. The guest agreed to pay for a room and sometimes a bed or even a candle (usually an extra charge was made for each item); the innkeeper agreed to prepare the guest's meal from the food the guest left at the front desk. But many innkeepers were so untrustworthy that guests often felt safer taking their meat to a local butcher for preparation instead.

At village or roadside inns, barmaids often received attentions from male customers. (Authors' archives, 18th century)

Guests who did eat at the inn dined in a smoky, foul-smelling kitchen run by the innkeeper himself or one of his wretched minions, often an older woman or even his wife. Everyone ate together—guests, innkeepers, servants, and muleteers. After the meal, guests usually tucked themselves away in bed, hopefully a straw one since it had fewer fleas than rag "mattresses." One 17th-century account of a night spent in a Spanish *venta* (inn) illustrates the problem:

> If I had been placed on my mother's doorstep, I do not think she would have recognized me, such was the strength of the fleas which attacked me. It was as if I had measles when I got up in the morning and there was not an inch on my body, my face, or my hands where there would have been room for another bite.

As sordid as these inns were, innkeepers formed cooperative guilds or informal associations for their common purposes. Established innkeepers, for example, wanted to stop or at least restrict foreign or nonlocal competitors who opened inns or taverns in towns that already had one or more. One way of undercutting these competitors was to forbid them from selling food or drink. Many a municipal law protected local tavern keepers in just this way, declaring the foreign establishments to be *hotels*—strictly speaking, rooming houses without license to offer meals.

Hotel law could actually be traced back to some centuries earlier. In 1254 French laws declared that only travelers could stay at hotels. Another in 1315 decreed that if a guest died at a hotel, the innkeeper had to pay three times the value of the victim's possessions. This latter edict was intended to discourage innkeepers from murdering their guests to obtain their property. In 1407 French innkeepers became bound by law to keep a guest register so that police could check for criminals and fugitives, as well as investigate the welfare of the naive traveler.

For many centuries travelers had found it safer and more congenial to put up in an abbey than to pay some cutthroat innkeeper for a "fleabag" on a cold and dirty floor. But in the years after the Reformation, many of the old hospices were closed, both Protestant and Catholic, or

As meeting places on roads or at ports, inns figured in many a true or fictional tale. (Advertising woodcut from True to the Core; A Story of the Armada, *London and New York, 1866)*

were converted purely to be used as hospitals. Gradually, as roads (especially post roads used by *mail carriers*) improved and traveling became easier and safer, innkeepers found that they could attract a good many paying customers. Increased commercial activity meant an ever-growing number of travelers and traders who sought lodging along the more popular roads leading to major cities. Coach travel became an especially big business in England where, by 1576, there were nearly 6,000 inns. Innkeepers in London led the way to new codes of professional ethics; they began to run clean, safe, and well-serviced establishments. During the course of the 18th century they established reputations as the world's premiere lodging hosts; countryside innkeepers eventually followed suit.

In early North America, proprietors opened new taverns, inns, and hotels, especially along postal routes and in seaports. The innkeeper had a more important place in the American economy than he had enjoyed previously or elsewhere. The Colonies and their important cities were widely separated geographically and culturally. Tavern keepers helped pull them together, offering appropriate places for commercial, political, and cultural exchange. Innkeepers were often prime gatherers of news and gossip, dispensing and even reading aloud newspapers and private mail to townspeople who convened at their establishments. They were so significant, in fact, that Massachusetts even passed a law demanding that every town support a local innkeeper and his business. In "long rooms" that held 10 to 15 guests, travelers of both sexes slept on the floor, with their feet near the fireplace and their heads resting upon their coats, which served as pillows. They usually ate in a community dining room at specified hours.

American innkeepers generally reaped fair profits. In Groton, Connecticut, during the Revolutionary era, 14 of the town's 15 area innkeepers earned higher than the average assessed income. Some were landed lords of considerable means. One innkeeper in Chester County,

Pennsylvania, owned 50 acres of land and held the prestigious title of *Esquire*. Some were professional people, one in Groton being a physician. Tavern keepers usually operated smaller establishments than innkeepers, offering food and lodging at cheaper rates. In early Colonial times they offered shelter for illegal gaming, but during the Revolutionary era they gave shelter to a more important clandestine activity—the development of plans to overthrow British rule and establish American independence.

Not all tavern keepers were men. Mary "Mollie" Sneden, who died in 1810 just before her 101st birthday, owned and operated a public house known as Cheer Hall in Palisades, New York. Licensed to "entertain travelers with all sorts of strong liquors," she had also ferried passengers (including Martha Washington) across the Hudson River beginning in 1753. She played an active role in the politics of the day and served as a spy during the Revolutionary War, although people have never quite agreed which side she spied on; some insist that she was a double agent.

In 1794 the City Hotel became the first in a long line of large luxury hotels to be operated in the United States. With 73 rooms, it soon became the social center of New York City. Similar lavish places were established in Baltimore, Philadelphia, and Boston. Their proprietors catered to high-class socialites, not to vagabond travelers. The Industrial Revolution increased leisure time and money, stimulated urban life, and created a vast middle class, all of which helped create the golden age of hotels. Resort hotels offered extravagant vacations for people with time and money to spend. The Hotel Tremont, which opened in Boston in 1829, was the first one whose proprietor was so courteous that he provided private rooms with doors that could be locked from the inside. It was also the first hotel to have *bellboys* (who were then called *rotunda men* and *room clerks*). It even had indoor toilets—another first. Innkeepers throughout the world copied such examples, as new concepts in hotel-keeping reshaped the profession into one that emphasized luxury and service.

The American West, especially San Francisco, became a center for saloon and hotel growth after the 1849 gold rush saw thousands of people flood the area in search of gold. Besides providing accommodations, the Western saloon-hotel was the major center of entertainment. Saloon keepers gained greater profits from the gaming and gambling opportunities they offered patrons than providing rooms and food could ever have generated.

By the end of the 19th century lavish hotels such as the Waldorf-Astoria in New York and the Palace in San Francisco stood as models for the world's innkeepers to emulate. In 1908 Ellsworth M. Statler opened the first modern commercial hotel in Buffalo, New York. It soon developed into an expansive chain of hotels designed to serve a new type of client—the motorist. Statler was the first hotel keeper to offer private baths, fire exits, free morning newspapers, and ice water. By the 1950's there were *motels* in which patrons could drive right up to the door of their room, thus alleviating the need for going through a main lobby and long hallways—and also undercutting the clients' need for *bellboys* and *porters* to carry their luggage and show them to their rooms.

From the beginning of the hotel movement, taverns and inns increasingly became eateries, and many converted former sleeping rooms into dining or storage rooms, or apartments. Others converted their space into establishments primarily for drinking. Whether known as bars, cafés, or pubs, these places generally served some modest food, such as sandwiches or pastries, but focused on the sale of alcoholic beverages, becoming social clubs of a sort. *Bartenders* developed their own distinct specialty, which involved skill in preparing a wide variety of drinks, as well as art in dealing with an extraordinary range of people at different levels of sobriety. Many taverns and inns were transformed into restaurants or bars as railroads took much of the traffic in the 19th and early 20th centuries, leaving the old roadhouses with

Inns were such central places that they were often polling sites; this tavernkeeper clearly has a preference for the Democrats. (From Harper's Weekly, *November 12, 1858)*

primarily local trade. That process was significantly speeded up with the arrival of automobiles, which bypassed many of the local taverns. Because people could cover the distances much more quickly by car, they needed to make fewer rest stops, for meals or for sleeping at night. Taverns along the old roads therefore lost much of their business.

Many hotel and saloon keepers, meanwhile, used their establishments as brothels as well as sleeping, dining, and gaming houses. In most countries and throughout history, prostitution has been a major attraction exploited shrewdly—often openly—by innkeepers. Although few innkeepers openly operate brothels as part of their businesses anymore, many are still involved in the prostitution business to some extent. Even the finest hotels in the world frequently offer prestigious "call girl" services to guests. And many hotels are still "fleabags" catering to drug dealers and alcoholics, as well as the mentally ill and indigent who have nowhere else to go.

Contemporary hotels and motels offer a wide variety of jobs to many employees. *Chambermaids* clean the rooms of guests daily; *janitorial staffs* clean the hallways and public rooms; there are *groundkeepers, check-in* or *desk clerks* to receive guests and properly register them, and *security guards, doormen, bellmen,* and *porters* in large downtown hotels. Many other kinds of employees less directly related to the hotel business are also found, such as *dining room* and *kitchen personnel, swimming pool lifeguards,* and *parking lot attendants.*

Today, about three-quarters of the world's professional "innkeepers" are large corporations. A few major companies and large city hotels have effectively monopolized the industry, operating ever-expanding chains of hotels and motels—in the cities, in the country, and along all the major highways. From being independent entrepreneurs, many innkeepers have become *managers* employed by large corporations. Among the management personnel are *day* and *night managers* and *assistant managers* who oversee general operations; day and night *auditors* who make sure that receipts and deposits related to the day's business are in line and properly recorded. There are special managers, where needed, such as *building maintenance managers, security managers, game* or *casino managers,* and *entertainment managers; convention* and *conference managers* are responsible for booking business conferences, political conventions, and other large groups, which frequently meet in on-premises conference rooms and convention centers.

Today's innkeepers are clearly more than providers of rooms to weary travelers; they also offer entertainment, relaxation, and fine dining—and sometimes just a convenient short-term retreat. Innkeepers also allow business employees to blend business with relaxation by offering them plush convention rooms accompanied by fine dining and lodging facilities.

For related occupations in this volume, *Restaurateurs and Innkeepers,* see the following:
 Butchers
 Cooks
 Prostitutes
 Restaurateurs
 Waiters

For related occupations in other volumes of the series, see the following:

in *Communicators*:
   Messengers and Couriers
in *Financiers and Traders*:
   Bankers and Financiers
   Merchants and Shopkeepers
in *Helpers and Aides*:
   Drivers
   Movers
   Private Guards and Detectives
   Servants and Other Domestic Laborers
in *Leaders and Lawyers*:
   Prison Guards and Executioners
in *Warriors and Adventurers*:
   Robbers and Other Criminals

Poulterers

Poulterers are those people who have prepared animals of the bird family for sale to the public. In ancient Greece, marketplaces were inundated with vendors of all sorts of poultry, the favorites being geese, doves, and partridges. Sales were quite high in the business, since Greeks rarely ate heavy meats like beef, preferring instead the lighter poultry. Even in Rome, where meat was much more readily consumed, poultry was still in great demand. A good Roman poulterer was certain to stock his roadfront counter or street carriage with geese, ducks, and peacocks. He killed the fowl at the time of sale, thus ensuring a freshness that was impossible for butchers to offer. (Animals such as cows, pigs, and sheep had to be slaughtered ahead of time, but the meat could not be preserved for long.)

All medieval cities had poulterers who roamed the streets selling their goods; some of the more prosperous poulterers even had shops. Since meat had become much more popular than poultry, *butchers* fared much better than poulterers and most of them, in contrast, could afford to operate from stationary shops. In China, wandering vendors regularly supplied restaurants and taverns throughout the countryside and in major cities with poultry, and particularly barbecued chicken—a longtime favorite. Some even had regular delivery routes.

As time went on, some of the larger cities had poulterer guilds. In 14th-century London poulterers' guilds lodged frequent and vehement complaints against foreign poulterers, who regularly flooded the city, free-lancing their goods for comparatively cheap prices. A 1345 edict in London was designed to stop "folks bringing poultry into the City" to market it in "lanes, in the hotels of their hosts, and elsewhere in secret." It forced them to take it "to the Leaden Hall and there sell it, and nowhere else."

Poultry has remained a popular food item throughout history. In a 16th-century work entitled *Italian Banquet* there are even instructions for a favorite court recipe of the

These Egyptian poulterers are plucking birds, while evidence of their handiwork hangs above them. (From History of Egypt, *by Clara Erskine Clement, 1901)*

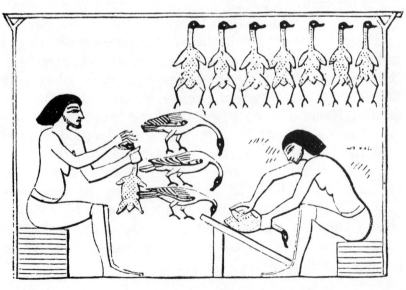

day; the recipe teaches the art of the flashy "making of Pies that Birds may be alive in them, and fly out when it is cut up." Eventually the slaughtering, preparing, and selling of poultry was undertaken by butchers and general *grocers*, until there were very few poulterers at all. Today, most commercial poultry is handled by butchers in their own shops or in general grocery stores, and innumerable laborers work to pluck and gut the birds for commercial distribution.

For related occupations in this volume, *Restaurateurs and Innkeepers*, see the following:
   Butchers
   Cooks
   Restaurateurs

For related occupations in other volumes of the series, see the following:
in *Financiers and Traders*:
   Merchants and Shopkeepers
in *Harvesters*:
   Farmers
   Hunters
in *Manufacturers and Miners*:
   Factory Workers

Prostitutes

Prostitution has been a part of human history long enough to have been given the half-serious designation of "the oldest profession." While that term is commonly used mockingly, reflecting prostitution's current lack of respectability and status, prostitution has often been included within the mainstream of other occupational skills. Even today, many prostitutes describe themselves simply as "working girls."

Prostitution is a relatively short-term profession that has historically been very hard on its practitioners. Physical attractiveness is an important qualification for success at the trade, either natural or artificially enhanced with wigs, makeup, and dim lighting. Age has always been the greatest enemy of the working prostitute, as well as the ravages of venereal disease (a fairly modern scourge that first reached epidemic proportions in the late Middle Ages), and pregnancy.

Prostitution has been a largely urban phenomenon, particularly associated with seaports and army encampments, where there were large numbers of single men. Both men and women have offered to engage in sex for payment throughout history, but prostitution is largely a woman's occupation. In a succession of male-dominated societies, it was one of the very few alternatives to domestic life as a wife and mother. Apart from unmarried women, or *spinsters*, women were generally either wives or prostitutes.

In many societies in the past, prostitution was seen as providing a necessary outlet for males. An argument frequently maintained in ancient Greece was that no man's wife would be safe unless citizens had recourse to prostitutes. In 17th-century West Africa a similar feeling led to tribal prostitutes being authorized and valued. The death of a tribe's public prostitute was an occasion of great lamentation and fear.

The beginning of prostitution as an occupation is impossible to pinpoint, but it seems reasonable to assume that it followed closely behind the development of the concept of payment for services rendered. Among the earliest references to it are those dating from the 18th century B.C. in the Bible. Tamar, a widow without children, masqueraded as a prostitute, as was accepted Jewish practice at the time. Her aim was to be impregnated by her father-in-law. She "put off her widow's weeds from her, and covered her with a veil, and wrapped herself, and sat in an open place." (Genesis 38:15) Her father-in-law, Judah, saw her, assumed she was a prostitute, and proceeded to barter with her for the price of her services. The transaction was not covert; it took place in the open and was clearly a well-established and unremarkable occurrence. Apparently prostitutes then were a distinct class of people, readily identifiable by their clothing. Some months later, when Tamar was discovered to be pregnant, Judah immediately ordered her

This view of the Whore of Babylon shows all the decadence and opulence normally associated with the profession. (By Albrecht Dürer, late 15th century)

burned for "having played the harlot"; only her revelation of his paternity restored her to grace. The double standard reflected here—acceptance of male patronage of prostitutes, while scorning the women engaging in it—was strongly fixed in Hebraic society and still forms a major part of Western attitudes. When Moses laid down the laws for his people in the 14th century B.C., he prohibited all Jewish women from becoming prostitutes. The men could use foreign harlots, but Hebrew women were supposed to be inviolable. Moses and his successors later tried to legislate against prostitution entirely, reacting against the foreign influences spread by exposure to them, specifically the worship of Baal and Moloch. Prostitution continued to flourish, however, and their attempts to outlaw it faded.

The religious connection with prostitution, which worried the Hebrew patriarchs, was widespread throughout much of the ancient world. In Babylon the worship of the goddess Mylitta included ritual *sacred prostitution* that was demanded of all women. Once in her life every woman was obliged to go to the sacred prostitute's precinct and offer herself to the first stranger who threw her a silver coin. After this one sacrificial offering of her body, the woman was free to get married and resume a normal life with absolutely no stigma attached to her. Herodotus recounted this practice in 480 B.C., but the worship of Mylitta was active as far back as 2000 B.C. Elsewhere in the Near East and Mediterranean, prostitution was included as part of religious obligations in the worship of Ishtar in Syria and Astarte in Phoenicia.

Many prostitutes in the ancient world practiced their trade as a means of making a living, with little thought about the sacred aspects of their work. For some it was a temporary expedient used to earn a dowry, a practice still followed by the Ouled Nail women in Algeria. In 1000 B.C. Solomon recounted the tale of a typical transaction conducted by a streetwalker outside his window. A youth was accosted by "a woman with the attire of a harlot, and subtle of heart. (She is loud and stubborn; her feet abide not in her house; Now she is without, now in the streets, and lieth in wait at every corner.) So she caught him, and kissed him, and with an impudent face . . ." propositioned him. The prostitute of Solomon's time was openly a part of city life, garbed in a distinguishing costume to advertise her availability and soliciting business much as a modern city prostitute does.

Prostitution was not a Western invention, of course. In ancient India it was also a widespread and, at least initially, a somewhat shadowy occupation. In the epic, the *Mahabharata* (about the time before 1000 B.C., though actually written down only centuries later), prostitutes were decried as evil creatures linked with gamblers and thieves as part of a disreputable subculture. Prostitution involving both boys and women was widespread in ancient China. In the Chinese system, all prostitutes were *slaves*, totally at the command of their owners. Women were considered to be of no value in Chinese society, and prostitution was one of the main ways that they could be put to use. Mythically, Chinese prostitution is supposed to have started in the dawn of history, during the time of the three emperors. The earliest concrete reference to it is from 650 B.C., when the emperor Kwang Chung took steps to set aside distinct districts for prostitutes in his cities, possibly to make regulation of the activity easier.

Greek and Roman Times

The high-water mark of prostitution as a mainstream career in the West occurred in classical Greece. During the golden age of philosophy and art that centered around Athens from roughly the seventh to fourth centuries B.C., many of the leading women in Greece were prostitutes. Respectable wives and mothers were confined to the maintenance of the household and rearing of children. Only prostitutes were able to develop their creative abilities and mingle with the leaders of the era.

There were four classes of prostitutes in ancient Greece. At the top of the profession were the *hetairae*, also known as the *foals of Aphrodite*. These were women of exceptional physical beauty, who combined driving personalities and intellectual attainments which the Greeks believed made them the worthy consorts of the leading thinkers, artists, and politicians of the day. A woman who succeeded as a *hetaira* could go far, indeed. Famous *hetairae* were able to amass great amounts of money and were accorded enormous social distinction. They were very uncommon prostitutes and could afford to be very choosy about the men they accepted as lovers, rarely consorting with more than one man at a time. Though the *hetaira's* social position was very lofty, her actual status under Greek law was tenuous. As a woman, she was denied citizenship and, to a large extent, had to rely on the protection of powerful patrons. By the fourth century B.C. the *hetairae* of Greece were organized in guilds that took collective responsibility for the conduct of their members. This did little, however, to protect the individual *hetaira*, who was at the mercy of any disgruntled lover who wished to sue her for the recovery of his money, often on the flimsiest of grounds.

This vulnerable position was made abundantly clear around 350 B.C. when Phryne, the most famous woman of her day, was brought to trial by an undistinguished former lover on the grounds that she had violated a 250-year-old Solonic statute against impiety. Phryne was a woman of immense wealth, who numbered some of the greatest names of Greece among her lovers. She was the model for the painter Apelles' *Aphrodite Rising from the Sea*, as well as the inspiration for Praxiteles' statue of the Cnidian Aphrodite. Her case was won for her by a leading orator, who stripped her before the court and bade it pity her state and remember her divine link with the goddess. The precedent thus set offered all prostitutes in Greece a modicum of protection under the law.

The second specialized class of prostitutes in Greece were the *auletrides*, women highly skilled in flute-playing and dancing. No formal or informal gathering of any importance was complete without its *auletrides*. Their performance did not necessarily include bedding afterwards, but the content of much of their repertoire was designed to arouse the audience. When the proper ecstatic height was reached, the *auletrides* would make themselves available for sex for a negotiated fee or a valuable present. The combination of prostitution and entertainment is one that occurs repeatedly throughout history, appearing in many different cultures.

The third class of prostitute in Greece included the ordinary whores, classified under the heading of *dicteria*. There were many more prostitutes to be found at this level than among the highly trained and respected *hetairae* and *auletrides*, but even the common practitioners of the trade could hope to advance upwards to those levels. The *dicteria* form an important landmark in the history of prostitution. They were established as a class in 594 B.C. by an edict of Solon, the Athenian lawgiver. In his ordering of society, Solon decided that the widespread and unregulated common prostitution of his day would work most effectively by being brought under municipal control. He organized the first legalized, city-run brothel system, which regulated the activities of the prostitutes it employed and set standards for their upkeep and location. Under the Solonic code, the *dicteria* were placed under the control of the city police in the port of Piraeus and confined to a recognizable district close by the shore, where they were easily accessible to the sailors who made the greatest demand on their services.

The personal appearance of the prostitute was mandated. She was required to wear brightly flowered robes that made her instantly distinguishable as a prostitute, protecting the wives and mothers of respectable citizens. In addition to this uniform, the common prostitutes generally dyed their hair blonde, or wore blonde wigs, and put on heavy face makeup to attract customers and hide age wrinkles or defects of their complexion. This professional trademark is still evident in Western societies.

With the institutionalizing and regulating of the prostitution industry in Athens, it became extremely lucrative and attractive to many enterprising businessmen to open their own *brothels*. Such owners were called *pornobosceions* (hence the present word *pornography*) and could make huge sums of money. Even though prostitution, as such, was not a fringe occupation in ancient Greece, with individual members of the profession sometimes achieving high status, the role of brothel owner had no such immunity from scorn and disdain. Any citizen found running a house of prostitution forfeited his citizenship. The lucrative nature of the business, however, assured that many *pornobosceions* actually were citizens operating at a distance under assumed names.

At the bottom of the social scale of prostitution in classical Greece was a class of unregulated, broken-down women who were ready to sell their bodies to anybody for a very meager sum. These women were disdainfully called *runners* or *she-wolves*, and included old women, the diseased, and the disfigured who had dropped from the higher ranks as they lost their physical attractiveness. Most of the runners were former *dicteriae*, but even *auletrides* and an occasional former *hetaira* could be found walking the streets at night in search of a client.

Unless a prostitute was able to make some monetary provision for her older years while she was working, descent into poverty and disgrace often accompanied her advancing age, as is true for most prostitutes even today. There was no security for a prostitute, even in the socially accepting climate of classical Greece. Once she had embarked on her career, there was no switching in midstream and hoping to attract a husband and settle into a domestic situation. The line between wives and prostitutes was clearly and inviolably marked.

The integration of prostitution into legitimate society was much more complete to the east of Greece, in early India. The earlier classing of prostitutes with thieves and gamblers apparently gave way to an acceptance of them as distinct and productive members of society. Eventually, prostitution developed into a largely hereditary caste in India, and as such was smoothly and fully integrated alongside other hereditary lower castes in the ordered heirarchy of existence. It was also an accepted occupation for widows, unhappy wives, and discovered adulterers. For all Indians, their *dharma* (life's duty) was laid down in their birth caste and had to be faithfully followed. Any person accepting his or her *dharma* and attempting to fulfill it was a good and productive member of society. Prostitution was without stigma, even though it was solely an occupation of the lower castes. Women of the three highest castes were forbidden from entering into it.

Succeeding rulers strengthened and enlarged upon the moral, religious, and philosophical framework of their unified social system. Prostitution became an unremarkable mainstream occupation and life-style. It even had its own complete textbook, the *Kama Sutra*, written by Vatsyayana around 400 A.D. And there were many distinct classes of Indian prostitutes, whose social status mirrored their ranking.

Prostitution was a very attractive alternative to the hard labor involved with maintaining a poor family's home or practicing a menial trade in poverty-stricken India. Unlike the Western prostitute, the aging Indian prostitute was not a social discard. She could honorably retire, marry her pimp, and raise a family of young prostitutes and pimps to carry on the family tradition.

Prostitution's position in Western society suffered greatly as the leadership of the Western world passed to Rome. The only prostitutes who were accorded any respect and status there were the highest class: the *delicatae* or *famosae*. These were the Roman equivalent of the *hetairae*, but lacked the exceptional intellectual and artistic training that had made the *hetairae* outstanding components of Greek culture. The *famosae* were ornamental and upper class in their manners and speech. Many were of good family by birth and took up the career for the monetary rewards or their own pleasure. They moved freely within high Roman society but were marked as being apart from it. A freeborn Roman man was forbidden by law from marrying a prostitute.

Rome became the first European society to institute registration of prostitutes for the purpose of taxation. The *vectigal*—the tax levied on prostitutes by all Roman emperors from Caligula in 37 A.D. to Theodosius in 390

A.D.—provided a massive income. The individuals who were compelled to pay the *vectigal* comprised only a fraction of the number of prostitutes who actually worked under Roman domination. Many prostitutes evaded registration because they were unwilling to pay the tax and took exception to the rules it imposed on their conduct. By law the prostitute was prohibited from wearing in public the modest *stola* that other Roman women wore. She was also forbidden to use the *fillet* which bound the hair, and could not wear the same type of shoes, jewels, and purple robes that other Roman women did. She had to wear a man's toga or a brightly flowered dress; dye her hair yellow or red; and wear sandals. In practice, some prostitutes found the dress code unconfining. They took to wearing transparent silk and gauze dresses imported from Asia and happily left behind the *stola*. The *delicatae* were exempt from this dress code, while the huge number of other working prostitutes defied comprehensive control.

Prostitution became an incredibly widespread and diversified industry, with practitioners to be found in every situation where there might conceivably be business. *Doris* were beautiful prostitutes who always appeared naked to solicit customers. The *lupae* (she-wolves) frequented gardens and parks and howled to attract trade. *Bustuariae* worked the graveyards and were often called on to act as mourners when they were between jobs. *Noctiluae* walked the city streets at night, while *forarie* were to be found on any country road. *Diabolaiae* were named for the cheap coin that was their going rate, but even they were better off than the *quadrantariae*, who would work for half the sum, or the *blotidae*, who were named after a potent and vile drink served in the lowest taverns. The *gallinae* (hens) were prostitutes who doubled as thieves.

Brothel keeping evolved into a highly specialized and distinct profession, the *lenocinium*, with subdivisions for different jobs within the industry. The *lupanarii* were the keepers of regular houses. *Adductores* and *perductores* were pimps who specialized in filling the specific requirements of moneyed patrons. *Concilatrices* and *ancillulae* were women, often older former prostitutes, who acted as go-betweens.

Prostitution was hardly restricted to the separate world of the brothel and professional pimp, however. The maintenance of prostitutes was regarded as a necessary part of business for a number of independent proprietors. The Roman public baths quickly became open brothels, with prostitutes of both sexes offering massage and further inducements to their clients. The linking of prostitution and massage parlors dates from this common Roman institution. Every tavern had a group of slave girls kept for the patrons' amusement; this class of prostitute was the *copa*. *Barbers* and *perfumers* also became synonymous with the *lenos* (bawds) who ran houses of prostitution, as they generally supplied girls or boys for their customers. Even *bakers* were notorious for using prostitutes called *aelicariae* or *baker's girls* to drum up trade. Imperial Rome, following the example of its emperors, was practically one great whorehouse. Prostitutes of both sexes were to be found throughout the structure of its society.

The rise of Christianity in Rome brought about a new view of prostitution. While other Romans may have considered prostitutes low class, Christians regarded them as sinful. Reclaimed prostitutes who were converted to Christ, however, could be fully redeemed, with the examples of Mary Magdalene, St. Mary of Egypt, St. Pelagia, St. Theodata, St. Afra of Augsburg, and many others testifying to the holiness of forsaking prostitution. In 305 A.D. the Council of Elvira formally excommunicated all harlots and strumpets from the body of the church, unless they married Christians and thereby renounced their trade. The official Christian view was that prostitution could not exist within a godly framework. The same council came down even more heavily on the large numbers of businessmen making their living from prostitution. The *procurer* and *panderer*

Mary Magdalene's conversion to Christianity inspired many attempts to save "fallen women." (By Albrecht Dürer, c. 1511)

were considered to be condemned to hell, never to be forgiven.

Early Christianity's strongest effort to restrict widespread prostitution was led by a former prostitute who had capped an amazing rise in society by marrying the emperor Justinian, ruler in Byzantium in the sixth century A.D. The empress Theodora had started her life as the daughter of an animal trainer in a circus. Her early career as an entertainer led her naturally into prostitution, where she used her wit and vitality to move into ever-higher circles until she finally claimed the emperor himself. She then gave up her profession and turned her efforts to reclaiming other prostitutes. She threatened pimps and panderers with the death penalty; she then gathered 300 prostitutes of the lowest sort and shut them in a convent under close supervision and prayer, trying to force their conversion. The deaths of several prostitutes who flung themselves from the walls after some months of confinement and the utter lack of interest shown by the rest of the captives doomed Theodora's efforts.

The Middle Ages

During the Middle Ages in Europe, prostitution was widespread but was looked upon as an evil occupation, reeking of Satan. The common prostitute was not indulged. Charlemagne exhibited a representative attitude when he imposed the penalty of scourging (severe whipping) for prostitutes and their pimps during his reign at the turn of the ninth century. At the same time, as so often happens, the strict morality decreed for the general population was hardly adhered to by those setting the standards. Many medieval monasteries and nunneries were notorious for the licentious freedom of their not-so-cloistered inhabitants. The rich and titled kept their *lemans* (mistresses) and concubines in a *gynaecea* reminiscent of an Eastern potentate's harem. Some of these were, in effect, high-class brothels for the gentry.

The succession of major wars of expansion known as the Crusades, as well as the many minor wars throughout medieval Europe, brought many prostitutes employment as *camp followers*. Accompanying the armies of marching men, they combined nursing, cooking, cleaning, and sex in a profitable and common occupation. The common man-at-arms welcomed the camp followers' attentions, but his leaders often found them to be intolerable nuisances to the discipline of their sprawling armies. In 1158 Frederick Barbarossa, the Holy Roman Emperor, decided that the situation had become intolerable. During a campaign through Italy, he decreed that any soldier consorting with a prostitute would be whipped and the woman would have her nose sliced off as punishment.

As Europe moved into the late Middle Ages, the ascendancy of large towns and cities actively embarking on a course of economic expansion affected prostitution. The occupation came to be viewed as a necessary evil that, since it could not be eradicated, should be run by the rich and the state in order to be profitable and orderly. The small-time pimp, procurer, and bawd found themselves outlawed. All too often their fate was to be condemned, tortured, or killed for attempting to operate on their own. Almost all European towns had a state or municipal brothel that could be monitored and controlled for the benefit of the public coffers. One of the most famous of these was set up in Avignon by the young queen, Joanna of Naples, in 1347.

Prostitutes were organized into guilds, following the lead of many other workers. Their guilds represented them and were responsible for the actions of individual members. Prostitutes were restricted to designated city areas that were given over to their trade. They were also required to wear distinguishing dress that marked them as prostitutes. In Avignon, prostitutes had to wear a red knot on the shoulder, but in other towns special headgear, sashes, or other brightly colored articles of clothing were mandated.

Municipal prostitution in the continental fashion never developed in England. The English were repelled by the notion that prostitution should be run by the government. Instead, British prostitutes found their customers in public baths, which were organized by King Henry II, late in the 12th century. Originally intended to be places promoting public hygiene, the baths, called *stews*, were in reality just brothels. The term *stew* became a general name for a prostitute until the 19th century. English prostitutes in the 1300's were a barely tolerated subculture often associated with thieves and other criminals. They were supposed to wear striped gowns or other distinguishing articles of clothing and stay within the confines of acknowledged districts under pain of punishment.

Municipal prostitution and the stews of England both faded from the scene by the middle of the 16th century. The increasing expense of their upkeep was part of the reason for their disappearance, but the main impetus was the appearance of a new and dread scourge, syphilis. Syphilis was first recognized and recorded as a disease in Italy in 1495, and spread with epidemic quickness throughout Europe. The Italians called it "the French sickness," the French named it "the Italian sickness," and so on; but its common and widespread name was "the whore's disease." Prostitutes found that their lives were greatly complicated by the ever-present spectre of a disease that was painful, disfiguring, and often fatal. It became inextricably linked with the profession and further lowered the already degraded status of the common prostitute. Starting in the 16th century, prostitutes in Europe were required to submit to periodic medical inspections that looked for evidence of rampant syphilis. This continued even when the municipal brothel had given way to privately operated whorehouses, run under the direction of a *madam*, a style that characterized much of European prostitution.

In 17th-century Restoration England, after the overthrow of the repressive Puritan rule, prostitutes flourished as they had never before. The formidable wit and artistry of English society's ablest minds turned to dramatic productions which mocked the moralistic conventions so dear to the Puritan creed. Sex was rampant, and affairs with other men's wives and prostitutes were seen as commonplace, complicated, and occasionally riotously funny.

Prostitutes found that the fashion of public masquerade that swept the English upper classes made it far easier for them to work. They commonly wore masks and dressed in fine clothing, making themselves indistinguishable from the similarly attired nobility. The anonymity of the masquerade enabled a lord to escort a paid prostitute to the theater or any other public place without fear of exposure and scandal. Prostitutes who associated with or were "kept" by men of the upper classes were also called *courtesans*.

The theater figured in Restoration prostitution for more than the opportunity for secret meetings it provided the audience. Actresses were often readily available for the watching gentry in return for a consideration—either a valuable present or plain payment. The highest pinnacle a prostitute could aspire to was to be a successful actress with a consequent entry into the boudoirs of the rich. From there the possibilities were enormous. Nell Gwynne was the most famous and successful actress/prostitute in English history. She parlayed her success on the stage to a succession of noble lovers of ever-increasing rank, and eventually found herself in King Charles II's

In a familiar fictional plot, the courtesan Formosa is blamed for leading young men to gamble and waste their lives in her posh villa. (Advertising woodcut from Formosa: Or, The Railroad to Ruin, *London and New York, 1869)*

bed. Immensely wealthy from the presents she demanded for her company, she became a popular folk hero throughout the land.

Following the royal example, lords and gentry could visit prostitutes without shame or public outcry. In the 18th century there developed a distinct class of cultured, discreet courtesans who catered to the rich and influential, had considerable status, and occupied the top of

Fashionable courtesans often had finely appointed houses and servants like this young Black page boy to wait upon them. (Engraving by William Hogarth, from Harlot's Progress II)

their flourishing profession in England. By the mid-1700's a form of prostitution that was popular in the capitals of the Continent made its appearance in London. This was a very elegant, refined house where a select contingent of prostitutes were under the complete control of a madam. The house catered exclusively to the monied members of Parliament and to rich noblemen.

An alternative for the monied patron was a system of *bagnios* (bathhouses), into which a gentleman would enter, scan the list of available women, and indicate his choice. She was then sent out for, and the pair would retire to her apartment or another suitable location. This arrangement anticipated the 20th-century *call girl* system made possible by the invention of the telephone.

The great majority of English prostitutes never reached the continental house or the *bagnio*. *Streetwalkers* of all ranks cluttered the streets of the cities. Taverns, too, retained their ancient tie with prostitution, serving as home bases and brothels. Several famous ones of 18th-century London were Bob Derry's School of Venus and the Golden Lion, nicknamed The Cat.

There was a tremendous subculture of criminality that existed in the teeming alleyways of London, and much of the common prostitution was conducted within its embrace. Prostitutes associated with thieves and robbers in disreputable inns throughout the city and acted as lookouts for profitable prey. Some of the women took a more active part in criminality. The popular and elegant masked balls were a boon to the many prostitutes who also worked as *pickpockets*. Blackmail was also a lucrative sideline, with rich provincials visiting the city a favored target. One oft-used ploy would find a pregnant prostitute working in concert with a male accomplice known as a *trapper*. He would confront a *mark* and accuse him of fathering the child. The threat of a summons of the police and subsequent embarrassment would almost invariably squeeze a sizeable sum of hush money from a frightened country squire.

The subculture of large-city prostitution employed great numbers of bawds, procurers, and pimps. *Bawds* were most often old prostitutes who could no longer make their livings by selling their own bodies. The bawd would work to find suitable clients for younger prostitutes she associated with, using aggressive salesmanship, deceit, or humor, as the situation called for. *Procurers*, male or female, supplied brothels with new recruits. The rigors of the trade quickly aged or diseased women working in the whorehouses, so there had to be a constant stream of replacements to satisfy the demands of the customers for fresh faces. By offering them a place to stay, food, and a steady income, the procurer would enlist girls to work in the brothel. Often the unwary target felt unable to leave once she had been lured within the brothel's walls. Once started in a life of prostitution, the young woman often felt unfit for any other life and remained without further pressure. The tactics of the 18th-century English procurer are still employed in large cities throughout the world. *Pimps* were special providers of custom-tailored services. They worked for the rich and prided themselves on finding prostitutes to fit the special requirements of their patrons.

In 1758 the Magdalen Hospital in London was founded to provide a place where reformed prostitutes could be treated for any disease that they had and find support in their attempt to leave the subculture. This attempt was more successful than the Empress Theodora's had been over a thousand years earlier. By 1786, nearly 2500 women had been admitted. This was a sizeable number but still only a small fraction of the tremendous numbers of women who were working the streets, parks, and theaters. To some, prostitution remained an attractive alternative to a life of unremitting toil and poverty as either a low-paid worker or wife and mother. There were glamorous examples of common women who had risen to wealth and prominence via prostitution, and it was the only occupation for women that offered even the faint hope of advancement.

The Far East

The prostitute's status was very different in the Far East. In China, entry into the profession was not a decision that women made for themselves. China's very stable and long-enduring culture was a totally male-dominated one that accepted prostitution as a matter of course. Public brothels had been licensed and set up by the state as early as the seventh century A.D. Prostitutes were slaves who were bought young and trained in singing, dancing, reading, and writing until they reached 14. At that point they went to work. As in other cultures, the most beautiful and accomplished prostitutes gained considerable prestige and led very comfortable lives, supported by rich and powerful men. The distinction between the marriageable woman and the prostitute that exists so strongly in Western society was clearly made in China, but for entirely different motives. A Chinese match was a matter of careful arrangement solely calculated in terms of monetary advantage and status. Love was reserved for the prostitute and concubine. Her position was hardly inferior to that of the lawful wife.

In the 19th century, prostitution flourished in many major Chinese cities. The standard place of business was a floating brothel known as a flower boat. These elegantly fitted-out houses of prostitution offered entertainment and the amenities of fine restaurant service for their clients.

In 17th-century Japan, before the onslaught of European and American contact, prostitution was a universally accepted and completely integrated component of social life. As in China, the man's honor was paramount, with women existing only to serve him. Prostitutes were purchased at an early age from their parents for a set time period of 10 or 20 years. They then went to work either in brothels maintained in special districts set up in the cities or at one of the many inns throughout the countryside that always offered prostitutes along with lodging for the night.

Music, dancing, and other performing arts were often associated with the provision of sexual pleasure, as with Japanese geisha girls. (From The New America and the Far East, *By G. Waldo Browne, 1901)*

There was no shame involved with a woman's working as a prostitute. What small guilt there was went to the parents who had sold her while she was still in infancy. The prostitute was looked upon as doing a noble deed by working at her trade and thus helping her parents. After she retired, she could marry and lead a normal life. In fact, the prostitute had an excellent chance of making an advantageous marriage upon her retirement. She was approximately 25 years old, well-trained, and had had the opportunity to meet many more eligible men than the woman who had stayed at home. This Japanese attitude toward prostitution changed in the 19th century after much exposure to Western attitudes of contempt and scorn for the prostitute. The ordinary prostitute was not treated as a social outcast, but her position as an admirable member of Japanese society was lost.

Modern Times

The massive industrialization of the 19th century in Europe and North America did little to diminish prostitution's attractiveness to some Western women, in spite of its low social standing. Female employment was severely restricted, with domestic service, sewing, and low-paid factory work practically the only occupations open to women. The self-sufficient rural family life that had been the mainstay of traditional values was increasingly diminished by the employment of husbands and fathers in exploitative factory jobs that were barely able to sustain a family. A woman who was left without even that meager support often moved into prostitution of necessity. A study of 2,000 prostitutes made in New York City in 1868 listed the following reasons for entry into the trade:

Destitution: 525
Inclination: 513
Seduced and abandoned: 258
Drink: 181
Ill-treatment: 164
As an easy life: 124
Bad company: 84
Persuaded by prostitutes: 71
Too idle to work: 29
Violated: 27
Seduced on an immigrant ship: 16
Seduced in an immigrant boarding house: 8

The seduction of immigrant girls and the forcible enrollment of them into the ranks of a brothel's prostitutes became much more widespread in the United States as immigration swelled at the end of the 19th century. This so-called *white-slave trade* roused tremendous public outcry, and legislation was enacted to prevent it.

In the United States as in Europe, prostitution centered around the cities, with a sharply defined hierarchy among its workers. The highest-priced prostitutes were refined and discreet about their business, most often operating out of elaborate *houses* or free-lancing and maintaining their own apartments. The cheaper prostitutes either openly walked the streets or lived in unpretentious brothels. Very often the brothel would be connected with a bar or saloon, with the prostitute urging patrons to buy expensive, watered-down drinks before retiring upstairs to a bedroom.

The profit that a woman could make working as a prostitute was the overwhelming reason the profession remained enticing. By the beginning of the 20th century it was not unusual for an active prostitute to earn from $50 to $400 a week, whereas a skilled *seamstress* or *domestic servant* would be fortunate to earn as much as $8. The inflated earnings of the prostitute rarely made their way into savings accounts. The expenses she had to meet were high enough to quickly siphon off any amount of earned income. A prostitute living in a brothel had to pay the madam exorbitant prices for her food and lodging and also had to spend a great deal for the clothing, hairstyling, cosmetics, and sundries that were necessary to present an attractive and salable image.

The prostitute operating on her own was in no better situation. Since she was working at a profession that was,

These young prostitutes are lolling around the house waiting for their night's work to begin. (From Women: A Pictorial Archive From Nineteenth-Century Sources, *by Jim Harter, Dover, 1978)*

at best, barely tolerated by the law, she normally had to pay two or three times the normal rental for her apartment. The world of the prostitute, entwined as it so often was with bars and other places where liquor and drugs were used, was very conducive to her own development of an addiction, which made prudent saving impossible. The same scenario is still completely current.

Police protection could also be a heavy drain on the prostitute's take. Laws forbidding solicitation and prostitution were in force throughout all of the United States, with the exception of New Orleans. The fame of that city rested as much on the glamorous attraction of its "red light district" of Storyville as it did on Dixieland

Prostitutes like this somewhat brazen young woman spent much of their private time in the company of other women. (From Women: A Pictorial Archive From Nineteenth-Century Sources, *by Jim Harter, Dover, 1978)*

jazz. In the 1870's more than 7,000 prostitutes worked in New Orleans, operating out of a huge number of bordellos ranging from sleazy tenements to opulent establishments. Prostitution was one of the mainstays of the city's economy.

Prostitution was essentially a profession of free-lancers and small-time entrepreneurs in the United States until the 20th century, when the immense potential profits attracted powerful underworld groups. Organized crime took control of all the highly lucrative prostitution to be found in big cities and resort areas, leaving very little for small-timers. Their control of prostitution tied in very well with some of their other very profitable activities. During the Prohibition era, large criminal organizations running the illegal liquor business also took over prostitution and often offered both side by side. Organized crime's control of the narcotics trade today provides it with an effective hold over many of the prostitutes it employs. Many prostitutes become addicted to heroin or cocaine and become totally dependent on their pimp to supply them. They turn over all their earnings to the pimp and allow him to make all decisions concerning their lives.

Prostitution in the United States is legal only in Nevada, where each county has the option to allow it. Churchill County, Nevada, is the only U. S. jurisdiction to have had a public referendum on the matter; prostitution was voted in by a two-to-one margin. Legal prostitutes there are fingerprinted and carry I. D. cards issued by the local police or the district attorney. Brothels are restricted to side streets, away from schools or churches. Prostitution is prevalent throughout the rest of the country, of course, but always operates under the shadow of illegality.

Prostitution is legal in various European localities, though often solicitation and the keeping of a house of prostitution are strictly prohibited. The ensuing harassment and clouded civil status caused prostitutes throughout Europe, though most cohesively in France, to unionize and form associations to lobby for better treatment. French prostitutes even called a nationwide strike in the mid-1970's to air their grievances.

The most vital example of the municipal prostitution that was common in medieval Europe is in the St. Pauli district of Hamburg, Germany, which is famous for its regulated bordellos. The municipal government provides strict overseeing of the sanitation and conduct of the prostitute and exacts a tax on her earnings. Even in Germany, though, traffic in the municipal brothels is slackening as many prostitutes free-lance and as suburban areas are becoming the centers of wealth.

Modern Japanese prostitution is indelibly linked with the image of the *geisha*. Geishas had been a part of Japanese society for hundreds of years, but their importance and popularity started to peak in the 1930's. The primary attribute of the geisha is her skill as an entertainer, with sex a coequal function. An apprentice geisha is adopted from her parents by an *okasan* (manageress) at a young age. This arrangement avoids a charge of slavery, the traditional relationship, while effectively maintaining the same bond. The young girl is trained in singing, music, deportment, poetry, and other skills until she is 14 or 15, when she becomes a full-fledged geisha. At that point the okasan acquires a master for her for a high fee. The master has the sole primary right to the geisha's body, but the okasan may still occasionally hire her out to other men. The most prized geishas live in monogamous relationships with their masters. Less fortunate geishas are prostitutes and entertainers with less control over their futures.

In the 1950's, after Japan's defeat in World War II, prostitution was officially abolished in Japan. This led to the development of the widespread patronage of *bar girls* (*B-girls*), also known as the "poor man's geisha." These women were prostitutes working as call girls and entertainers in nightclubs who were available for sex after the show.

The changing patterns of international wealth and

This idealized geisha dedicated herself to pleasing her lover. (British Museum, c. 1768)

power have led to the resurrection of white-slavery rings that specialize in the luring or abducting of young girls into enforced prostitution. A significant number of young European women, runaways, and others answering ads promising glamorous jobs as hostesses, are ending up as prostitutes in the Middle East. The biggest financial gain for organized international procurement rings is currently to be found in oil-rich Middle Eastern capitals.

But however much societies have changed, the practice of prostitution has remained essentially unchanged throughout the centuries. While some societies, such as the 20th-century communist societies of China and Russia, claim to have completely halted the activities of prostitutes within their borders, such campaigns generally simply turn prostitution into a clandestine trade.

For related occupations in this volume, *Restaurateurs and Innkeepers*, see the following:

Bakers
Innkeepers
Restaurateurs

For related occupations in other volumes of the series, see the following:

in *Healers* (forthcoming):
  Barbers
  Nurses
in *Helpers and Aides*:
  Bath Workers
  Undertakers
in *Leaders and Lawyers*:
  Lawyers
  Police Officers
  Political Leaders
in *Performers and Players*:
  Actors
  Dancers
  Musicians
in *Scholars and Priests*:
  Monks and Nuns
  Priests
in *Warriors and Adventurers*:
  Gamblers and Gamesters
  Robbers and Other Criminals

Restaurateurs

The profession of modern-day *restaurateurs*—owners and operators of restaurants—has developed through a history of the public serving of foods by *tavern owners, cookshop keepers*, and even *innkeepers*. Early tavern keepers were probably in the business of serving drink chiefly, although some scant provisions of food may have been offered as well.

Tavern keepers in ancient Greece operated large and thriving businesses in the main towns and seaports. Most were run by male citizens who made extensive use of slaves to supply the labor and loose women to offer entertainments of the lowest kind to customers. Greek tavern keepers were a rugged sort. They had to deal with the crudest villains, criminals, and roughnecks of society, who frequented their establishments. The keepers were often social outcasts themselves, who were constantly in trouble with the law for harboring fugitives and hosting illegal gaming and prostitution within their establishments. While Greek tavern keepers offered some foodstuffs, drink was their specialty. None could hope to operate honest businesses, because no decent Greek citizen would go to a tavern or any public eatery.

Citizens instead formed "eating clubs," whereby a group of men would take turns hosting dinner at each other's homes for the others in the group. In this way they all got to eat out frequently without using the vulgar public or commercial places. In many ways the dinner or *symposium* (dinner followed by usually serious conversation) host—even though purely an amateur in his approach to the evening's events—was more closely related to today restaurateur than ancient tavern owners were. The private host made all the arrangements for the meal. He invited the guests; told his cooks and servants what to do, how to do it, and when; and even bought most of the food himself—a job regarded as too important to entrust to a slave or houseboy. The guests (always male) arrived in formal wear, including their best sandals, having specially bathed and perfumed themselves for the occasion, and spent the evening into the late hours enjoying the hospitality of their host. There was no way that public taverns or restaurants could compete with so intimate, tidy, and common a practice.

The Romans continued the same practice of dining at one another's homes on a rotation basis. They went even further than the Greeks by routinely offering not just dinner but full-scale banquets—with each trying to outdo the other, especially when political or business favors were sought. Women were sometimes allowed to attend these private dinners, but usually just for cheap entertainment or company in return for a free feast or other favor.

Taverns were generally avoided still. Although there were many inns, only desperate travelers or the roughest transients would frequent the dingy restaurants that the

Early Roman cookshops were often open to the street. (From Museum of Antiquity, *by L.W. Yaggy and T.L. Haines, 1882)*

innkeeper often operated in conjunction with his lodging business. Of restaurants in Rome, most were the cookshops that offered "fast foods" from boiling stewpots set on open street counters. These were generally operated by lower-class men, who often hired a *cook's boy* or two to help with the food preparation, serving, and sometimes even advertising. The owners of these shops or stalls set up business in the midst of the marketplace or business districts; there they tried to entice shoppers and workers to buy ready-to-eat cooked peas or sausage. Their best customers were workmen. Many poor people also frequented these shops because they could not afford stoves and rightly feared the threat of fire that they posed. Since poor people often could not afford to buy ready-cooked foods, the enterprising cookshop operator would cook food that customers brought to his establishment, reducing their cost for a meal while increasing profits for the shop. Many cookshop operators even sold boiled water by the potful so that people could rush home with it to cook their meals.

Cook's boys were sent into the streets as vendors with small trayloads of stews and other foods. The owner of such a business cared little about the stench associated with his shop, which elicited the complaints of emperors and slaves alike, nor about the quality of food he served. Few people dared to guess what his stews consisted of, not to mention the bugs and contamination that floated freely into the open cauldrons as they sat atop charcoal fires. The Emperor Hadrian once had this to say about Florus, a nobleman who lowered himself by attending taverns "cheek by jowl with cut-throats . . . thieves, runaway slaves, hangmen, and coffin makers":

> Florus would I never be,
> Now a-tramp to taverns he,
> Sulking now in cook-shops see,
> Victim of the wicked flea.

Gradually, however, some actual restaurants began to appear in Rome. The owners of *cauponae* (eating houses) served decent food to sober tradesmen. They had little tables and chairs and countertops so the customers—mostly men—could eat inside the establishment, rather than carting their bowls about town or eating on city streets. *Thermopolia* (hot-drink establishments) were popular spots for drinking *calda*, a diluted wine mixed with herbs and spices and then heated. (There was no coffee or tea in Rome.) There were even some splendid restaurants that served only the highest classes of people. These were located at the public baths, and their owners were often middle-class citizens. For the most part, though, restaurants, taverns, and cookshops were avoided by self-respecting Romans. The operators and keepers were despised, regarded to be on the same level as thieves and prostitutes.

In the Dark Ages following the decline of Rome, public eateries fell into general disuse as European society regressed into a system of self-sufficient manorial estates, where money was no longer even a common medium of exchange. The first signs that the profession of *restaurateur*—broadly including all owners and keepers of public eateries and drink establishments—was being revived came from the East. It was in that part of the world that the only active, large-scale commerce was being carried on. Large caravans of camels and traders carried silks and exotic spices such as pepper and herbs from China, Japan, and India to Islamic trade centers, such as Baghdad and Damascus, and from there to Europe, often through Arabian middlemen. Many restaurants sprang up along these trade routes.

The first such European establishments were opened in Spain, a major region of entry for traders from the East. Most of the restaurants on these caravan routes and highways were grimy and sordid, as well-known for their dealings in prostitution as in food and drink. The successful owner of such a place was certain to have abundant stocks of water and wine—the water for the beasts of burden, who became dehydrated along their desert treks, and the wine for the hardy and equally deprived trader. The shopkeeper had to be rugged and

These Chinese restaurateurs have set up a rice stand near a military station. (From The New America and the Far East, *By G. Waldo Browne, 1901)*

worldly to deal with these travelers—brash and thieving as they were, and prone to excesses in drinking, gaming, and fighting.

The finest restaurants in the world during the Middle Ages were in China. Marco Polo once observed that the operators of the *wine shops* (taverns) and public eating places there were very imaginative in their resources. Not only did they save every scrap of meat and by-product for their cooks to use, but they even made an expensive delicacy of blood, heart, kidney, and lung soup—a specialty in the Kaifeng eateries. Cheap restaurants in Hangchow and elsewhere catered to working people. They offered cheap, deep-fried buns, but the wines to wash them down were very expensive, and represented the restaurateurs' real profit margin. Some operators even hired porters to make deliveries of food to homes or business places. Most Chinese restaurants were open late at night to serve government workers and administrators, who customarily put in long hours. All-night shops, collectively known as "the night market," catered mostly to lower class and poor people. Those restaurateurs running higher-class places often supplemented their profits by operating take-out sheds in the back. There poor people lined up to buy the remains of the dishes of the rich in the front room.

Eating utensils and furniture were important acquisitions for the operators of these Chinese eateries. The presence of porcelain or silver usually indicated that the restaurant was rather elegant, especially if benches were used as well. (Tables and chairs were rarely used because they could not hold as many people as benches could.) Some restaurants even continued the tradition of floor seating only, to fit the largest number of people into a crowded space.

Some restaurateurs demanded that their customers, usually all males, be properly dressed, but those whose primary purpose was to offer illicit gaming and prostitution rarely imposed any restrictions or demands on customers. Part of the job of restaurateurs at such establishments was the procuring of and caring for the prostitutes. They were well treated, enjoyed free meals, and lived on-premises or in adjacent housing.

Restaurateurs in China operated many convenient wine shops serving quick meals to single diners. They also ran specialty restaurants, such as noodle shops or laborers' shops. Some did professional catering on the side—preferably in the daytime when shop business was slow. Funerals and boat banquets were among the many affairs that they were hired to cater. There were 72 "first-class shops" (*cheng-tien*) in Kaifeng alone, and scores of teahouses in Hangchow. In fact, there were so many of every type of restaurant available that competition became bitter. Many shopkeepers advertised that certain well-known officials had once dined at their places, or did so regularly. Some furnished their establishments with lavish decorations, famous paintings, beautiful indoor gardens, and fine silver. Most advertised their food as being "fine," while their competitors' was "rough." But no matter what gimmick or finery the restaurateur employed, the amount of business he attracted was generally dictated by the quality and manners of his prostitutes. At the Shop of Humane Harmony outside of Kaifeng, guests were enticed by literally hundreds of women, who offered free wine at the entryway. Like many similar restaurants, it was referred to as a "mountain," because once guests made large purchases of wine on the main floor, they were permitted to advance to the upper floors, where hundreds of other prostitutes offered more than wine.

Tavern keepers in European cities of the Late Middle Ages engaged in similar practices, but virtually none offered either fine food or atmosphere. Their first concern was in properly staffing prostitutes. After that, the thoughtful tavern keeper would make sure that only thin candles were available for lighting—and not too many of those. Dim lighting was greatly appreciated by patrons, who hid behind benches and tables busily engaged in the illegal tossing of dice or playing of cards. The third order of business was to make sure that the wine was of good quality and properly priced before the *wine inspector* dropped by. This was important, since *wine criers* had to be stationed outside the tavern, letting the public know the prices and inspection reports concerning the tavern's wine business.

Baked-meat sellers operated quick-food shops in most medieval and Renaissance cities of Europe. They were a crude and unscrupulous lot, generally considered to be in the business of food poisoning. Closely related to this group was the *cookshop operator*, who served food to be eaten in the shop or to take out, or who cooked food brought in by customers. Public cookshops had been around for several centuries, but became especially prosperous as feudalism declined, when people began moving into towns and cities and a monetary exchange system was revived.

As early as 1183 there was a public cookshop in London. It catered, as most restaurants did at the time, to travelers. Few townspeople were so poor that they would eat at such a disease-ridden place. Being little concerned with repeat business, the entrepreneurs of these establishments would serve slop at any stage of rot, knowing that the traveler had nowhere else to turn for a meal. The cookshop keeper and his employees threw bones, by-products, and all manner of undesirable things onto the floor of both kitchen and dining area, creating the most awful stench and disease-breeding conditions that could be imagined. Thoughtful restaurateurs sometimes eased the bad odor by adding daily doses of sweet-smelling basil and southernwood to the decaying garbage. Food was handled with dirty hands and was exposed to diseased fleas from city rats and river sludge, as well as to the casual licks of domestic pets.

Most tavern and restaurant keepers were more concerned about stocking good wine than good food. Even at that, keepers trying to hold down costs stored and served wine in nauseatingly smelly pigskin containers, rather than use good wooden barrels. Meat pies were the most common food, but nobody could be sure where the restaurateur had procured his "meats," or how they had been handled or prepared afterwards. One Pablos of Segovia, before eating a restaurant's or cookshop's meat pie, used to cross himself and say a silent prayer for the soul of the human body that he presumed had been butchered and minced into its contents. It was commonly accepted that the flesh of condemned and executed criminals made a perfectly good ingredient for commercial shops, where overhead had to be kept at a minimum. We can only wonder exactly how much of the restaurateur's profits lined the pockets of *undertakers, prison guards*, and *executioners*.

Among the first restaurateurs who catered to local populations rather than travelers were the operators of coffeehouses. The atmosphere that a coffeehouse's operator could establish was far more important than the coffee or tea (which had only recently begun to come in from the East) or foods that he served. The coffeehouses became social, intellectual, and business centers of many an English city, and their popularity quickly spread to the Continent and to the New World. Keepers of coffeehouses were often rather eminent gentlemen; they tried to get notable writers, statesmen, and artists to frequent their establishments, regarding this as the best way to keep a faithful and steady clientele. As smoking became popular, some enterprising operators offered free clay pipes to guests. Many great works of literature, political tracts, and philosophies were drafted and discussed in critical circles at these very coffeehouses. Many of their operators were better known for their literary critiques and advice than for their business accomplishments. Some were downright pained at having to spend so much time with the business that their academic and literary pursuits suffered.

Restaurateurs had always focused on serving travelers, but they frequently lost business when travelers provided themselves with pack and convenience foods. These were items, such as dried meats, that travelers could take with them so that they would not starve if caught in a vast wilderness or desert. Convenience foods were very popular in America, where there always seemed to be a new wilderness to traverse. Restaurateurs in new frontier cities such as St. Louis, Kansas City, and San Francisco often complained bitterly that their business suffered from the abundance of *pemmican* (a dried buffalo meat that lasted for months) and other such foods, which many pioneers preferred (probably for the sake of their cheap price, rather than for their taste) to the finer restaurant meals. Traveling Asian traders used an especially convenient and always fresh food source. At night, after their camels (or sometimes horses) had watered, the men would pierce the beasts' veins and suck their blood. On some routes, traders did this regularly, but tried to do so in controlled patterns so that they would not kill the camel.

The restaurant business was often closely and sometimes intimately connected with the lodging business. Before the Industrial Revolution, few cities could support a restaurant that had nothing to offer but dinner. In fact, the word *restaurant* was first used only in 1765, when a Parisian soup vendor named Boulanger opened a shop offering *restaurants* (restoratives), such as soups and broths. He was one of the first proprietors to offer a choice of dishes listed and priced on a written menu. Still, most people preferred eating at home. Rich people had their own cooks and middle-income people cooked at home. Taverns sometimes served as restaurants, but since they primarily provided lodging for travelers, they are discussed separately in the article on innkeepers.

After the French Revolution a great many renowned and talented Parisian chefs lost their jobs as private cooks in aristocratic households. They sought employment instead in the increasingly popular public restaurants, of which there were over 500 in Paris alone in 1804. Restaurateurs were happy to employ the disenfranchised chefs, and they vied bitterly to get the finest in the trade. They then advertised their fine chef and the foods and menus he prepared. The restaurant business not only increased from this new fame and publicity, but it also became more prestigious and high class. French restaurateurs paved the way for a new look and unprecedented respect for their profession. Antoine Beauvilliers opened the modern world's first truly luxurious restaurant, and many French hotels hired restaurant operators to run elaborate and highly departmentalized kitchens. Magnificent French restaurants of the 19th century featured armies of laborers, all specializing in the minutest of kitchen and service details.

The serving of public meals to local communities first became a big business in the 19th century. The Industrial Revolution resulted in large urban centers with dense populations of wage earners, who had more money in their pockets than the traditional farm worker or artisan ever had. Moreover, as the workday grew shorter, many workers enjoyed more leisure time than ever before. The

The coffee stall is always a welcome sight for workers in the early morning. (By Gustave Doré, from London: A Pilgrimage, *1872)*

times were finally right for restaurateurs to open the doors to large, legitimate dining rooms for families. Prostitution and gambling were left to only the meanest and basest operators in the profession, as gentlemen—and even women and children—were courted by the new-style restaurateur. Not all restaurateurs ran particularly pleasant eateries, however, as may be surmised from the following description of a London chophouse, taken from Robert Surtees' 1854 novel, *Handley Cross*:

Now for a chop-house or coffee-room dinner! Oh the 'orrible smell that greets you at the door! Compound the cabbage, pickled salmon, boiled beef, sawdust and anchovy sarce. "Wot will you take, sir?" inquires the frosty waiter, smoothin' the filthy, mustardy, cabbagey cloth, "soles, macrel, vitin's—werry good boiled beef—nice cut. Cabbage, cold 'am and weal, cold lamb and sallard."

Only in modern times have restaurants come to be frequented by the rich and powerful. (From Gems From Judge)

Hah! The den's 'ot to suffocation—the kitchen's below—a trap-door vomits up dinners in return for bellows down the pipe to the cook. Flies settle on your face—swarm on your head; a wasp travels around; everything tastes flat, stale and unprofitable.

By the beginning of the 20th century many socialites in the Western world had become accustomed to dining in restaurants, country clubs, spas, and resorts. Eating outside of the home had become a pastime for the elite, rather than a sordid necessity for the poor traveler who was without choice. Restaurateurs in major cities all over the world struggled to make their establishments ever more refined and lavish, offering sumptuous and exotic dishes, lively and elegant atmosphere, and top-notch service. With the advent of the automobile, many restaurateurs pioneered the idea of luxurious country dining. Many a villa, chateau, and old inn or tavern were converted into beautiful eateries combining cosmopolitan menus with country charm. To serve diners of more modest means, many restaurateurs ventured into the cafeteria business after World War I. The idea of self-service public eateries had first appeared in San Francisco during the gold rush of 1849, when there was a critical shortage of restaurateurs available to handle the demand for dining service.

Today restaurateurs operate all kinds of eateries, from drive-in quick stands and trailer diners to palatial multiroom eateries with gardens, live entertainment, and extraordinary (both in quality and price) bills of fare. Smaller restaurants offer employment only for the restaurateur, one or two *waiters* or *waitresses* and perhaps a *cook*. The largest establishments have entire staffs of workers and specialists. Although the kitchen and dining room workers in such places are numerous, the staffs are not nearly as large as those in similar restaurants of the 19th and early 20th century. Many restaurateurs today in America and other industrialized nations work as franchisees, operating one of a corporate-owned large chain of "fast-food" restaurants catering to middle-class families and working people. Even in Communist China, small private restaurants are once again springing up, in a bow to individual enterprise.

Among the many jobs associated with restaurant work are the following: *waiters* and *waitresses*, who directly serve patrons; the *maitre d'hotel* (often referred to as the *maitre d'*) who arranges large dining affairs and often acts as the direct supervisor of the dining room staff; *hosts* and *hostesses*, who arrange and direct seating and table settings; *cashiers* and *food checkers*, the latter used in cafeteria and self-service restaurants; *busboys* and *girls* (so-called, although they may be of all ages—even elderly), who clean tables and serve water and coffee; *runners*, who fetch whatever any other workers need; *chefs* and *cooks*, some of whom specialize in particular items such as sauces or pastries; *food and beverage controllers*, who monitor the costs of stocks; the *steward*, who is in charge of food storage and issuance; and a *wine steward*, whose specialty is managing the restaurant's wine cellar and sometimes purchasing wine; the *decorator*, who prepares fancy hors d'oeuvres and canapés for banquet rooms; *food production managers; menu makers*; the *prep man* or *woman*, also called a *pantry worker*, who prepares salads, fruit dishes, juices, and dressings; the *vegetable cleaner*; the *dishwasher*; the *porter* or *janitor*; and finally, the *restaurant manager*, who supervises the total operation of the restaurant. Some of the largest and most lavish restaurants even staff their own *bakers* and *butchers*. In the smallest operation, of course, all of these jobs might be taken on by one or only a few persons; in the largest, numbers of people fill each and every slot.

For related occupations in this volume, *Restaurateurs and Innkeepers*, see the following:
   Bakers and Millers
   Butchers
   Cooks

Innkeepers
Prostitutes
Waiters

For related occupations in other volumes of the series, see
the following:
in *Financiers and Traders*:
    Bankers and Financiers
in *Helpers and Aides*:
    Movers
    Servants and Other Domestic Laborers
    Undertakers
in *Leaders and Lawyers*:
    Inspectors
    Prison Guards and Executioners
in *Warriors and Adventurers*:
    Gamblers and Gamesters

Waiters

Waiters and *waitresses* are servers of food and drink, carrying them from the kitchen, pantry, fountain, and bar to the tables or hotel rooms where a restaurant's clients are dining. In ancient times servers were usually slaves placed in teams headed by a *chief server*. They worked mostly in the private homes of their masters, as well as in palaces and temples. Sometimes they worked for an *innkeeper* or *tavern owner*, who was well enough off to afford them.

As public eateries and taverns became more commonplace in medieval and early modern times, hired waiters or waitresses were used occasionally. More frequently, though, the serving was done by the *cook, baker, innkeeper*, or *restaurateur*; one person, or at least one family, often functioned in all of these roles. When waiters were used, they were typically of such low class and so grimy that starving travelers were known to lose their appetites at the sight of them. Usually only the loosest of women in the profession worked as *wine servers* or *barmaids*, and many of them doubled as *prostitutes*. In China, waiters called *gong heads* or *callers* had to memorize lengthy food and drink orders. If they forgot or made a mistake on any items, they were scolded rudely in front of their patrons and sometimes even docked in pay.

The profession of serving food is most closely derived from that of household servants, which were common throughout modern history. The grand middle and upper classes of the British empire of the 19th century were perhaps the best-known employers of domestic workers, including *kitchen servants*, who acted as food servers during mealtimes. A popular book of the day, *Domestic Management*, instructed household mistresses on how to handle and instruct the servants. In one place, it mentions one of the chores allotted to the *footman*—a carriage escort and livery stablehand, who also helped wait on tables at dinnertime.

> If he is ordered at dinner to break the claw of a lobster, he is not under any circumstances to crack it between the hinges of the dining-room door. He must take it at once into the kitchen, where force can be applied out of earshot of the master and mistress.

All house servants labored for long hours, both day and night, for nothing more than room and board and a very meager yearly allowance.

Stagecoach inns and hotels used waiters not only to serve tables but also to work as yard and luggage boys. By the late 19th century restaurants had become big business, and waiters and waitresses were needed to provide adequate service in them. More than one of these servers—then as now—ran a small restaurant of their own on the side, often stocked partly with meat, fish, and fine produce filched from their employer's establishment.

Waiters often take a great deal of verbal abuse from the customers they serve. (From Punch, or The London Charivari, *1870)*

They have always been a minority, however, and waiters and waitresses generally have been extremely hard-working, good at handling people (especially at pleasing them in anticipation of larger tips), and patient, as everyone who deals with the public must be.

Today people in the profession still tend to work long hours for small salaries, but they frequently make substantial earnings in tips and gratuities from satisfied patrons. In some parts of the world, notably in Europe, tips are added automatically to the price of the meal. Many of them work only part-time to augment salaries from other work, or when laid off or between regular jobs, particularly if their main jobs are of a free-lance nature. Full-time workers in large establishments are often protected by labor unions and minimum wage scales. When restaurants or dining rooms are associated with hotels, some food servers are employed to provide *room*

service—that is, to serve customers in their rooms rather than at tables. Sometimes restaurants have a *headwaiter*, called a *captain* or *maitre d'hotel*, whose job is to arrange banquets and supervise the staff of waiters and waitresses.

For related occupations in this volume, *Restaurateurs and Innkeepers*, see the following:
    Bakers and Millers
    Cooks
    Innkeepers
    Prostitutes
    Waiters

For related occupations in other volumes of the series, see the following:
in *Helpers and Aides*:
    Movers

Winemakers

Winemaking is the process by which the juice of a fruit is fermented to make an alcoholic drink. Although wine has been made from such things as currants, blackberries, dates, and dandelions, it is the grape that has been used most widely throughout history. The making of grape wine became the focus of a large industry, while the other types of wine were made mostly in the home, for private consumption. The people who oversee the making of the wine, who decide when to pick the grapes and which grapes to use, and who supervise each stage of the production of the wine are usually called *winemakers* or *vintners*.

No one knows where or how the first vintners made their wine. The earliest knowledge we have of vineyards and winemaking comes from Egypt and Mesopotamia, and the trade seems to have been fairly well established by 3000 B.C. The people of both these regions were for the most part beer drinkers, but wine was held in high esteem by the upper classes. It is likely that most vineyards were located on the estates of the wealthy and of the temples.

The method of pressing grapes used by the ancient Egyptians is still used in some regions today: they were trodden. The grapes were placed in jars or vats that were large enough to hold from one to four or more people. Treaders often held onto beams or ropes placed above the jars, since it can be difficult to retain one's balance when walking in grapes up to the knee.

Once the juice was pressed from the grapes, it was placed in jars to ferment; finally the jars were stoppered with mud. These jars were often labeled with information as to the contents of the jar and their quality. It is interesting to note that, even in that time, both the vintage year and the name of the vineyard were considered important information.

Though wine was made in many areas of the eastern Mediterranean, it was in classical Greece that winemaking first became a widespread profession. It is probable that the knowledge of winemaking spread from Egypt and Palestine into Greece, where for a long time it remained a local industry, the product of subsistence farming. With the rise of trade within Greece and with its neighbors, wine began to play a more important role. Indeed, *potters* benefitted greatly from the popularity of wine. Many of the *amphorae* (jars) that have survived from early Greek times originally held wine for distribution at home or around the Mediterranean. Greek wines were held in high esteem—some more than others—and the wine trade began to be rather profitable. People on larger estates began producing wine, and sending an increasing percentage of the product to market.

Probably the most important innovation in the winemaking process during this period was the Greek invention of the screw press around the second century B.C.

While some Egyptian workers pick the grapes, others (at the top) hang onto ropes to keep their balance while trampling the grapes. (From The Pictorial Sunday Book, *19th century)*

Before this, the crushed grapes were pressed by a wooden beam upon which heavy stones were hung. The screw press not only reduced the amount of physical labor involved in obtaining the juice, but it also was more effective in getting juice out of the grapes.

During Roman times the winemaking trade spread greatly. Wherever the Roman legions went, the natives tended to acquire a taste for wine. In addition to the many planted acres in Italy, vineyards and wineries sprang up in North Africa, Spain, and especially the southern regions of France. As the wine trade grew more profitable, vineyards became larger and larger, with an ever-increasing percentage of the farmland given over to vines. Wine became so profitable that during the second century B.C. the return on an investment in vines was greater than that for any other crop. This large-scale production of wine is illustrated by the large capacity of the presses and the size of the wine cellars found in the excavation of Pompeii.

Wine was taxed by the Roman government and the tax was often paid in kind—that is, in wine. This practice necessitated the existence of one of the most renowned wine-related professions. The government employed expert *wine tasters* to make sure that the tax was not paid with inferior wines.

With the rise in the size of vineyards, the winemaking trade gradually emerged as separate and distinct from that of vine-growing. The investment necessary to a large winemaking operation was very great. Many vineyard owners found it difficult to tie up their money in wine that had to be aged for some time before it could be sold. They preferred to sell their crop on the vine to a vintner who specialized in making the wine, and so get an immediate return on their investment.

The Romans were the first vintners to use wooden casks to any great degree for the storing of wine. In the modern winery, casks play a very important role in the aging process. Also important to the modern winemaker are the glass bottle and cork stoppers. Both of these were used in a very limited way by the Romans, though it is not known whether they understood the importance of these three innovations in the production of wine.

During the Middle Ages the wine trade was reduced in scope due to the difficulties of trading during that time. Amazingly, very little of the knowledge of winemaking seems to have been lost in this period. As with much other knowledge, the monasteries probably played a major role in preserving the trade. Some historians note that the number of vineyards that survived was much too great for the Church to have held them all. Monasteries did have large holdings of vine, however—for producing ceremonial wines, if nothing else—and monks did contribute to the revitalization of the profession. One has only to note that many of the most respected wines at this time came from monastic wineries.

From Roman times to the onset of the industrial age there were few changes in the mechanics of winemaking. The winepress that was used by the 16th-century Frenchmen would have been familiar to a Greek vintner of the first century B.C. The most important advance in winemaking during the Middle Ages came with the almost universal adoption of the wooden cask for the storage and transport of wine. The cask was important in the production of the wine because the porous wood allowed for better oxygenation of the wine. Also during transport the losses due to breakage were much less with wooden casks than with their earthenware counterparts. Glass bottles and corks did not come into general use until the 15th century. The importance of both lies in the fact that they allow the wine to mature properly without spoiling. The cylindrical bottle as we know it today began

In Europe, the innovation of barrels gave wine a special flavor. (From Food and Drink: A Pictorial Archive From Nineteenth-Century Sources, *by Jim Harter, Dover, 1979)*

to be used in the late 17th and 18th centuries. At first glass bottles were used as decanters for temporary storage after the wine had been drawn from a cask. The growth of the use of the bottle for storage is illustrated by the fact that by the end of the 18th century there were around two million bottles made annually in the Bordeaux region of France.

The use of the still to make alcohol, a development that came to Europe from the East in the late 13th century, opened up many new avenues of experimentation in the making of wines and wine-based products. The fortification of wine involves adding distilled alcohol to fermenting wine and thereby bringing to a halt the fermentation process. This method produced a sweet wine and had the added bonus of raising its alcoholic content as well. Distillation also gave rise to many other beverages such as the many types of brandies, as well as standard liquors, such as rum and gin. In this period winemakers began to develop and refine their products, especially the distinct regional wines of France. The experts who judged which grapes to use, when to pick them, and when to proceed to each new stage of the winemaking process were granted high esteem, especially in France. There the government in modern times has increasingly codified standards and quotas for the various regional wines, the pride of the country; and the judging of vintage wines has become something of a national pastime.

Today winemakers work not only in Europe and the Mediterranean region but in many other parts of the world as well. There are vineyards and wineries in North America, South America, South Africa, China, Japan, Australia, and New Zealand. Wine is made virtually anywhere that the grape will grow.

Modern vintners have a wealth of information about the chemical processes that are involved in turning out a good wine, which their predecessors did not have. They have all the advances of modern science at their disposal to help them in their work. Winemaking has become a very scientific and industrialized business. *Chemists* are employed to test the grapes for sugar content and acidity, so the growers will know the best time to pick them. Every stage of the pressing and fermentation process is monitored closely. At almost no time, from when the grape is picked until it appears on the table as wine, does it come into contact with the human hand. Miles of piping connect presses with huge oaken storage barrels. Bottles move on conveyor belts and are filled and stoppered automatically. It has reached a point where a modern French vintner has said—with some exaggeration—that it did not matter what kind of a growing year it had been for the grape; he could always produce a wine of the best quality.

For related occupations in this volume, *Restaurateurs and Innkeepers*, see the following:
  Distillers
  Innkeepers
  Restaurateurs

For related occupations in other volumes of the series, see the following:
in *Artists and Artisans*:
  Glassblowers
  Potters
in *Scholars and Priests*:
  Monks and Nuns
in *Scientists and Technologists*:
  Alchemists
  Chemists

Suggestions for Further Reading

For further information about the occupations in this family, you may wish to consult the books below.

General

Chang, K.C., ed. *Food in Chinese Culture*. New Haven: Yale University Press, 1977. A very thorough look at the role of food in Chinese life in all periods of history.

Hampe, Edward C., Jr., and Merle Wittenberg. *The Lifeline of America: Development of the Food Industry*. New York: McGraw-Hill, 1964. Follows the growth of chain stores, food distribution centers, grocery stores, and supermarkets.

Heiser, Charles B., Jr. *Seed to Civilization: The Story of Food*, 2nd ed. San Francisco: W.H. Freeman, 1981. A look at food's role in the evolving history of human civilization.

Henisch, Bridget Ann. *Fast and Feast: Food in Medieval Society.* University Park, Pennsylvania: Pennsylvania State University Press, 1977. An interesting account of the place of food in medieval society.

Quayle, Eric. *Old Cook Books: An Illustrated History.* New York: E.P. Dutton, 1978. A fascinating account of the various ways that food has been prepared throughout history.

Tannahill, Reay. *Food in History.* New York: Stein and Day, 1973. A colorful and readable history of food, its preparers and purveyors.

Brewers, Distillers, and Winemakers

Hyams, Edward. *Dionysus: A Social History of the Wine Vine.* New York: Macmillan, 1965. A good general treatment, emphasizing drinking more than winemaking.

Seward, Desmond. *Monks and Wine.* New York: Crown, 1979. A useful treatment.

Tudor, Dean. *Wine, Beer and Spirits.* Littleton, Ohio: Libraries Unlimited, 1975. Contains a good bibliography.

Innkeepers

Lathrop, Elise L. *Early American Inns and Taverns.* New York: Arno Press, 1968. A look at the Colonial food and lodging business as it helped to shape the American way.

Lundberg, Donald E. *The Hotel and Restaurant Busi-*

ness, 3rd ed. Boston: CBI Publishing Co., 1979. A review of one of the world's largest industries.

Prostitutes

Addams, Jane. *A New Conscience and an Ancient Evil.* New York: Macmillan, 1923. A crusader's exposé, yet excellent for the state of American prostitution in the early 20th century.

Bellocq, E.J. *Storyville Prostitutes: Photographs From the New Orleans Red-Light District, circa 1912.* Boston: New York Graphic Society, 1970. John Szarkowski, ed. Visually descriptive of the clothing and appearance of its subjects.

Bullough, Verne, and Bonnie Bullough. *Prostitution: An Illustrated Social History.* New York: Crown, 1978. A full and entertaining history of the subject, covering all aspects of prostitution from religious to social to medical.

Henriques, Fernando. *Prostitution and Society: A Survey*, in 3 vols. London: MacGibbon & Kee, 1962-68. An encyclopedic treatment. Volume 1 covers Primitive, Classical, and Oriental; Volume 2 treats Europe and the New World; Volume 3 views Modern Sex.

Pinzer, Maimie. *The Maimie Papers.* Old Westbury, N.Y.: Feminist Press, 1977. Ruth Rosen, ed. Revealing and informative letters of an American prostitute, 1900-1922.

Index

Acton, Eliza, 16
Actresses, 118
Adductores, 112-13
Afra of Augsburg, St., 113
Agora (marketplace, Athens), 4-5, 24
Alewives, 19
Amphorae (jars), 152
Annona (public handouts), 7
Anti-Saloon League, 80
Apelles (painter), 108
Appert, Nicholas, 56
Apple sellers, 63
Arrack, 77
Assistant managers (hotel), 96
Auditors, 96
Augustus (emperor), 46

Bagnios (bathhouse), 120
Bakers, vii, viii, 1-17, 39, 42, 59, 144, 147; brewers and, 20; commercial, 12-13, 15-16; and prostitutes, 113
Baker's girls, 113
Bar girls (B-girls), 128
Barbers, 113
Barmaids, 148
Bartenders, 94
Bawds, 113, 116, 121
Beauvilliers, Antoine, 141
Bellboys, 93, 94
Bellmen, 96
Bishops, 11
Black Death, 28
Book of Trades, 14-15
Bordellos, 127, 128
Bouncers, 88
Brewers, ix, 2, 19-20
Brewmasters, 21
Brid, John, 9
Brothel owners, 109-10, 112-13

Brothels, 95, 109-10, 113, 116, 117, 125; high-class, 115; public, 122; taverns as, 120
Buckingham, Duke of, 42
Building maintenance managers, 96
Burghers, 11
Busboys/girls, 144
Butchers, viii, 23-38, 59, 100, 101, 144

Calda (beverage), 134
Caligula, 6, 111
Call girls, 120, 128
Callers, 148
Camp followers, 115-16
Canteen girls, 62
Captains (restaurant), 150
Caravanserais, 89
Carter, Robert, 13
Carters, 59
Cashiers, 144
Casino managers, 96
Cauponae (eating houses), 135
Chambermaids, 95
Charlemagne, 115
Charles II, king of England, 118-19
Check-in clerks, 95-96
Chef bonnet (*gros bonnet*), 54
Chefs, 48, 50, 53-55, 140-41, 144
Chemists, 56, 156-57
Chief servers, 147
Christianity, 113-15
Cities and towns, 11, 15, 52, 68, 141; butchers, 27-28; and inns, 89; and prostitution, 104, 116
City Hotel (New York City), 93

Coffee merchants, 62
Coffeehouse operators, 139
Columbus, Christopher, 32
Concilatrices, 113
Confectioners, viii, 17, 39-43
Conference managers, 96
Convenience foods, 139-40
Convention managers, 96
Cookbooks, 33, 49, 50, 51
Cooks, ix, 11, 23, 26, 33, 45-57, 59, 134, 143, 144, 147
Cook's boy(s), 133, 134
Cookshop keepers, 131
Cookshop operators, 133-34, 138
Costermongers, viii, 59-65
Courtesans, 118-20
Cow keepers, 68, 71, 80
Crime: organized, 127; and prostitution, 120, 127
Crusades, 115-16

Day managers (hotel), 96
Dairy operators, viii, 59, 67-75, 80
Dairy workers, 39
Decorator(s), 144
Delicatae (prostitutes), 111, 112
Demosthenes, 4
Derry, Bob, 120
Desk clerks, 95-96
Dharma, 110-11
Dickens, Charles, 35
Dicteria (prostitutes), 109, 110
Dietitians, 56
Dining room personnel, 96
Disease, 7, 25, 28, 33, 36; prostitution and, 117; venereal, 103-4, 117

163

Dishwashers, 144
Distillers, ix, 77-81
Diviners, 3, 87
Domesday Book, 20
Domestic servants, 125, 148
Doormen, 96
Doughboys, 9, 16
Durer, Albrecht, 49

Edward III, king of England, 28-29
Entertainment managers, 96
Escoffier, Georges-Auguste, 54
Executioners, 139
Eyting, Sol, 54

Factory workers, 21, 56
Family occupations, 68, 84
Farley, John, 51
Farmers, 2, 59, 61, 68, 70, 73
Fishfags, 84
Fishmongers, ix, 63, 83-86
Food adulteration, contamination, 7-8, 16, 28, 29, 42-43, 63, 134, 138; dairy products, 69-70, 71, 72, 73
Food and beverage controllers, 144
Food checkers, 144
Food merchants, 62-63
Food preservation, 56, 62, 63, 67, 74, 84, 99; meats, 24-25, 30, 32-33
Food production managers, 144
Food vendors, 4, 59-60, 63, 64, 99, 138
Footman, 148
Foremen, 6
Frederick Barbarossa, 116

Gamblers, x
Game managers, 96
Geishas, 128
Gilpin, Robert, 13
Glasse, Hannah, 50
Glasse, Mrs. Hannaly, 33
Gong heads, 148
Government regulation, x, 51, 63-64; bakers and millers, 7-8, 9, 17; butchers, 28-29, 34, 35-36; liquor industry, 79-80; prostitution, 109, 116, 128; winemaking, 156
Grain merchants, 13, 14
Greengrocers, 62
Grocers, viii, 59-65, 101
Groundkeepers, 95-96

Guilds, 8, 27, 28, 32, 90-91, 100, 108, 116
Gwynne, Nell, 118-19
Gynaecea, 115

Hadrian (emperor), 134
Hamilton, Alexander, 79
Hawthorne, Nathaniel, 52
Head cooks, 49
Headwaiter(s), 150
Henry II, king of England, 116
Herodotus, 106
Herring girls, 56
Hetairae (foals of Aphrodite), 107-8, 109, 110, 111
Hinduism, 24
Hospices, 89, 91-92
Hosts, Hostesses, 144
Hotel keepers, 95
Hotels, 91, 92, 93-94, 95, 96, 148
Household servants, 125, 148
Human flesh vendors, 27, 139

Ice vendors, iceman, 64
Industrial Revolution, 13, 20, 32, 33, 56, 63, 93, 141
Innkeepers, ix-x, 31, 89-97, 134, 140, 147
Inns, 12, 51, 87, 88, 92, 94, 131, 132-33, 148

Janitorial staffs, 95
Janitors, 144
Jennings, Josiah A., 71
Jews, 104-6
Joanna of Naples, 116
Justinian (emperor), 114

Khans, 89
Kiddler, Edward, 40-41
Kitchen personnel, 96
Kitchen servants, 148
Knackers, 29
Kwang Chung (emperor), 107

Labor unions, 36, 128, 149
Lambe, Patrick, 12, 50
Langueyeurs, 29
Lemans (mistresses), 115
Lenocinium, 112-13
Lenos (bawds), 113
Liquamen (sauce), 47, 56
Lupanarii, 112

Madam(s), 117
Maitre d'hotel, 144, 150
Managers (hotel), 96
Marcus Apicius, 47

Marks, 120
Mary Magdalene, 113
Mary of Egypt, St., 113
Mary the Jewess, 77
May, Robert, 49
Mayenne, Duke of, 31
Mechanization, 14-15, 16, 20, 43; dairy products, 74, 75; distilling, 80-81
Menu makers, 144
Metics, 46
Milk carriers, 68
Milk score, 68
Milk sellers, 68-69
Milk walk(s), 68
Milkmaids, 69, 75
Milkmen (milk boys), 71-72, 75
Millers, vii, 1-17
Monasteries, monks, 20, 115, 154-55
Money lenders, 87
Moonshiners, 81
Morris, Helen, 52-53
Moslems, 78-79
Motels, 94, 95, 96
Municipal prostitution, 116-17, 128
Murrell, John, 49

Night managers (hotel), 96
Nightingale, Florence, 53
Nott, John, 50
Nutritionists, 56
Nutt, Frederick, 42

Okasan, 128

Panderers, 113-14
Pantry maids, 11
Pantry workers, 144
Parking lot attendants, 96
Pasteur, Louis, 74
Pastry chef, 54-55
Pastry cooks, 40
Pastry-master(s), 40-41
Paul V, Pope, 30
Peddlers, 26-27
Pelagia, St. 113
Pemmican, 140
Perductores, 112-13
Perfumers, 113
Pharmacists, 62
Phryne, 108
Physicians, 3, 87
Pickett, Albert J., 71
Pickpockets, 120
Pig keepers, 80
Pimps, 113, 116, 121
Polo, Marco, 136

Pornobosceions, 109-10
Pornography, 109
Porters, 94, 96, 136, 144
Potters, 152
Poulterers, viii, 99-101
Prep man/woman, 144
Priests, 23
Prison guards, 139
Procurers, 113-14, 116, 121
Prohibition era, 80
Prostitutes, x, 103-30, 148
Prostitution, 95, 129, 135;
    legal, 127-28; as
    profession, 103, 104-5,
    125-27; restaurants and,
    136-37, 142
Public baths, 113, 116-17, 134
Publicans, 21
Puestos, 62
Puritanism, 117

Quick cook(s), 55-56

Raffald, Elizabeth, 41-42
Ratcatchers, 32
Refrigeration, 33, 35, 64, 70,
    71, 74, 84
Restaurant managers, 144
Restaurants, 50, 94, 132-33,
    137, 140; commerce and,
    135-36; cooks, 51, 54-55
    (*see also* Chefs); public,
    140-41; waiters, 148-50
Restaurateurs, ix, x, 47-48,
    50, 59, 131-45, 147;
    French, 140-41
Revenuers, 81
Robbers, 88
Room clerks, 93
Room service, 149-50
Roosevelt, Theodore, 36
Rotunda men, 93

Rundell, Maria, 51
Runners (prostitutes), 110
Runners, 144

Sacred prostitution, 106
Saloon keepers, 94, 95
Saloons, 87, 94, 125
Sauce chef, 54-55
Sawyers, 13
Seamstresses, 125
Security guards, 96
Security managers, 96
Seneca, 46-47
Shambles (slaughterhouses),
    28-29
She-wolves (prostitutes), 110,
    112
Shopkeepers, 3
Short-order cook(s), 55
Sinclair, Upton, 36, 37
Slaughterhouses, 28-29, 34-35
Slaves, 11, 47, 60, 69, 79,
    147; as bakers and millers,
    3-4, 6; as cooks, 45-46,
    49; as prostitutes, 107,
    122
Sneden, Mary "Mollie," 93
Snow pits, 62
Solomon, 106
Solon, 109
Soyer, Alexis, 52-53
Spice-grocers, 62
Spice merchants, 59-60
Spinsters, 104
Spit-boy, 46
Statler, Ellsworth M., 94
Stewards, 144
Stews (baths), 116-17
Stills, 77, 79, 81, 156
Streetwalkers, 120
Supervisors, 6
Surtees, Robert, 142-43
Swimming pool life guards, 96
Symposium(a), 132

Tabernae (inns), 88
Tavern keepers, 87, 88, 92,
    93, 131-32, 137-39
Tavern owners, 147
Taverns, 12, 87, 92, 94-95,
    132-33, 134, 136, 140, 147;
    and prostitution, 113, 120
Tax-farmers, 32
Tea merchants, 62
Teamsters, 88
Test kitchens, 56
Theodata, St., 113
Theodora (empress), 114-15,
    121
Theodosius (emperor), 111-12
Thermopolia, 136
Trajan (emperor), 6
Trappers, 120

Undercooks, 49
Undertakers, 139

Vatsyayana, 111
Vectigal (tax), 111-12
Vegetable cleaners, 144
Vintners, 151-57

Waiters, ix, 143, 144, 147-50
Waitresses, 143, 144, 147, 149
Washington, George, 79
Washington, Martha, 93
Wellington, Duke of, 54
Whiskey Rebellion, 79, 81
White-slave trade, 124, 129
Wine criers, 138
Wine inspector, 138
Wine servers, 148
Wine shops, 136, 137
Wine stewards, 144
Wine tasters, 154
Winemakers, ix, 151-57